TEEN FINANCE UNLOCKED

BUDGET, SAVE, INVEST, BUILD CREDIT & TACKLE ADULTING LIKE A PRO

KATHY FREELAND

CONTENTS

INTRODUCTION

"If you make one dollar, you can make a million more."
@Tradeclass

You've just landed your first job. Maybe it's babysitting, mowing lawns, or flipping burgers at the local diner. You get that first paycheck, and suddenly, the world feels full of possibilities. A new phone? Those killer sneakers? Or maybe saving up for your first car? But hang on a second. Before you blow it all on concert tickets or a fast food run, let's delve into a subject that might not seem as exciting at first glance but is incredibly crucial: the art of managing money wisely.

This book is about making these money concepts simple and easy to understand. Thus empowering your journey toward true financial independence. This book is your ultimate playbook for mastering money management with ease. It's tailored for where you are right now, just starting out. We'll cover real-life concepts like saving, budgeting, and investing. We'll also cover some more difficult yet crucial concepts, such as taxes and insurance. We will explain them in an engaging and straightforward way to understand without all the complicated financial jargon.

Why should you care about money management concepts now? Well, here's the deal: Only about 16% of teens understand basic financial concepts. Understanding money management will allow you to be more in control and capable of making wise financial decisions. It will also help you avoid costly mistakes, such as overspending, racking up debt, and not planning for emergencies.

This book will show you how to start small but think big—your financial habits today will shape your financial success tomorrow. The only way to master the management of money is by learning the rules. If you skip learning how to manage money now, you might end up in a tricky financial predicament down the road. Let's face it, being in the top 16% of any class is a recipe for success.

Hi there! I'm Annie Whit, your financial guide on this journey. I've spent years helping people like you figure out how to make their money work for them. My goal? To make sure you don't feel like you need a dictionary just to read this book. I love breaking down complex money concepts into bite-sized, easy-to-understand pieces. I'm super excited to share what I've learned with you.

Money can feel overwhelming. Who hasn't cringed at words like "interest rates" or "credit scores"? But here's the thing: financial literacy isn't just for adults or Wall Street types. It's for everyone, especially you. You might have just started working for the first time and brought home your first paycheck. We will first show you how to understand a few things and answer some common questions, such as:

- Why is my paycheck smaller than I expected? What are all these taxes and deductions on my pay stub? (e.g., federal taxes, FICA, and Medicare) mean
- How do I turn this check into spendable money?
- What should I do with the money I do not spend?
- Should I get a credit card right away?

- ...and much, much more!

This book will help you cut through the jargon and get to what really matters: how to manage your money smartly.

We've packed it with a lot of real-life scenarios and interactive elements. You won't just read about money—you'll take action with your money. There are practical exercises to try out, quizzes to test your knowledge, and activities that make learning about money almost as fun as spending it.

We'll start with the basics, like understanding your paycheck, setting up a budget, paying your expenses, and saving the rest. Then, we'll move on to cool stuff like investing and digital finance. Don't worry; we'll take it step by step. By the time you finish this book, you'll not only understand how money works—you'll already be making smart moves with it.

I encourage you to actively engage with this material. Immerse yourself in the exercises provided, reflect on your spending patterns, and initiate discussions about your financial discoveries with friends and family. Money management is a universal aspect of life, making it an essential topic of conversation. Moreover, tackling these lessons collectively can significantly enhance the learning experience.

I hope that by the book's end, you will be on the road to financial independence with a clear vision of your financial goals. You're in control of your money, making wise choices, and feeling confident about your future. This book is your first step towards making your financial dreams a reality. So, let's begin this journey to financial empowerment and independence. You've got this!

1

MONEY BASICS AND UNDERSTANDING YOUR MONEY GOALS

Ever find yourself daydreaming about all the things you could buy with your first paycheck? Maybe it's the latest smartphone or those limited-edition sneakers everyone's been talking about. But then reality hits: you've got to make that cash last until your next payday. Welcome to the real world, where money doesn't grow on trees, and budgeting isn't just a word adults use to ruin your fun. This chapter is all about setting up a solid financial foundation. We're talking about understanding money beyond just spending it and why having a handle on your finances means less stress and more freedom to do what you love.

Let's start with a fundamental truth: money is more than just paper and coins. It's a tool that keeps life organized, but instead of organizing your music playlist, it **organizes your opportunities**. Money allows you to make choices, from buying that new game to saving for a car or even investing in your future. Think of it as a ticket that lets you trade for goods and services, whether it's grabbing a burger or paying for a concert. The choices are yours, but understanding how to wield this tool is key. Understanding these fundamentals is crucial to managing your money and achieving financial success.

The **power of money lies in its ability to influence decisions**. With great power comes great responsibility. This means making thoughtful decisions about how you spend and save. But be warned, the value of money isn't static. Ever heard of *inflation*? It affects how much your dollars will buy over time. Let's use this example. Let's say you have $5 today. What can you buy with $5? Two gallons (1/8 tank) of gas for your car or perhaps an ice cream sundae. Ten years from now, that same 5 dollars will not stretch nearly as far. Maybe it will only buy one gallon of gas or a single candy bar. That is what inflation is. Inflation almost always happens over time, but by how much it really cannot be predicted. But knowing how inflation impacts your purchasing power is critical to how you spend, save, and grow your money.

Then, there's *currency fluctuation*. Sounds complex, right? But it's simple: not all money is created equal across the globe. If you've ever traveled, you know that $10 won't get you the same amount of gelato in Italy as it does pizza in Chicago. Understanding these concepts helps you grasp why money's value shifts and why it's crucial to keep an eye on these changes when planning for big purchases or trips.

Gone are the days when all money was cold, hard cash stuffed in a piggy bank. Now, money comes in many forms. Ever paid using your phone? This is called *digital payments*. From credit cards to mobile apps like Apple Pay and Google Wallet, transactions are faster and often more secure than carrying around cash. Then there's cryptocurrency—Bitcoin, anyone? These digital coins are shaking up the financial scene, adding another layer to our understanding of money.

It's easy to dismiss money matters as adult problems or boring economics, but being savvy about finances now sets you up for success later. Setting financial goals can seem daunting, but knowing how to manage money means avoiding the common mistakes that lead others into debt or financial stress. Think of it as unlocking levels in a game; each level mastered opens new opportunities and adventures.

Understanding money equips you with the tools you need to make informed decisions—whether that means saving for college or planning a gap year adventure. Armed with knowledge, you'll avoid pitfalls and set yourself up for financial triumphs. Ready to take charge and build a foundation that supports your dreams? Then, let's start this exciting journey into the world of finance together!

SMART SAVING: GOALS, METHODS, AND MOTIVATION

You're eyeing that sleek bike at the store, the one that's practically calling your name. You imagine cruising down the street, wind in your hair, freedom at your fingertips. But wait, how do you get from dreaming to riding? It's all about **saving** early, and here's why it matters more than you think. Starting young with your savings might not sound thrilling, but trust me, it's like planting a money tree. The seeds of **compound interest** grow your savings over time. Imagine your initial stash of cash as a snowball rolling down a hill, picking up more snow—er, money—as it goes. The earlier you start rolling that snowball, the bigger it gets.

Then there's the **emergency fund**, your financial safety net. It's not just for adults to worry about. What if your phone screen shatters or you need a last-minute gift for a friend? Having an emergency fund means you're prepared without having to beg or borrow. It's like having a superhero cape tucked away for when you need it most.

Setting saving goals is where the magic begins. Think of it like plotting waypoints on a map. Without them, you're just wandering. First, figure out what you want in the short term—like that bike or concert tickets—and what's on the horizon for the long haul—maybe college or starting a business. Use the SMART criteria: **S**pecific, **M**easurable, **A**chievable, **R**elevant, **T**ime-bound. S.M.A.R.T. goals help you create goals that can help you have desired outcomes in a desired time period. For example, instead of saying, "I want to save money," try saying, "I'll save $300 in six months for a new guitar." That's a goal with a plan. Using this method will make it simple for you to develop simple actions to support a specific goal. For example, you could take action steps, such as saving $15 weekly for 24 weeks (6 months). This would come to $360, $60 more than you need for that guitar!!!

Now, let's talk about how to save without feeling like you're missing out on fun. Automatic transfers to savings accounts are like putting your savings on autopilot. Set it up once, and watch those savings grow without lifting a finger. If you're up for a challenge, try the **52-week saving challenge**. Week one, save $1; week two, $2, and so on. By the end of the year, you'll have over $1,300 saved without breaking a sweat.

Sometimes, we need a little inspiration from others who've been there and done that. Take Emma, for example. She started saving at 16 by babysitting and cutting back on daily coffee runs. Her goal? College tuition. By the time she graduated high school, she had saved enough to cover her first year without student loans. Or consider Jake, who wanted to start his own business by the age of 20. He saved diligently throughout high school using these same strategies and launched his first small business right after graduation.

The real win here is financial independence. It's not just about having money; it's about having choices and freedom. When you save smartly and start early, you're setting up the "future you" for success. Financial independence isn't just for adults; it's for savvy teens like you who know that every dollar saved is a step closer to freedom.

Saving might seem like a sacrifice now, but it's an investment in your future dreams and adventures. Each dollar you save today is a building block for tomorrow's opportunities. You don't have to be rich to start saving; you simply have to start. No matter how small, every effort counts toward achieving those big goals you've set your sights on.

UNDERSTANDING NEEDS VS. WANTS: MAKING SMART CHOICES

You're walking through the mall, and suddenly, there it is—the latest video gaming gadget calling your name. Your heart races, your fingers itch to swipe your debit card, and that inner voice whispers, "You deserve it!" But hold up a sec. Before making that purchase, let's discuss the difference between needs and wants. **Needs** are those crucial things you can't live without—like food, shelter, and clothing. They're the basics that keep you going day to day. **Wants**, though? They're the fun stuff: entertainment, luxury items like those designer sneakers you've been eyeing. You'll need to understand this difference when you learn more about managing your money. But hold that thought for now; we'll return to this concept during budgeting.

For now, though, just know that just because something is a want rather than a need doesn't mean you shouldn't indulge. That's where prioritizing comes into play. We will teach you how to create a spending plan, prioritize needs first, and then allocate additional funds for the FUN STUFF you want.

A real-life example of planning for needs vs. wants while saving

Let's say you earn $200 a month from a part-time job, have a few bills, and have a few splurges on which you would like to spend your money.

Step 1: The first step is always to cover your needs ($80) in order of priority. Evaluate each purchase's necessity by asking yourself: "Do I need this to survive or thrive?" If it's not essential or aligned with long-term goals, maybe it can wait.

1. Phone Bill: $40
2. Gas and Parking: $40

Step 2: Allocate at least 20% ($40) for savings, especially if you build up your emergency fund.

Step 3: That leaves a whopping $80 for wants. Go ahead and splurge on that Macha iced latte or the new beauty product you want. Better yet, throw more into your savings so you can take that trip to Italy with your friends next year.

Take note of the 50/30/20 rule. 50% of your take-home income can be used for expenses (Less is better!!). 20% for savings and 30% for wants. What happens to the rest? You can split between savings and wants. Impulse buying is like that sneaky friend who convinces you to stay out late even when you have an early morning class. It's fun at first, but it can derail your plans fast. Recognizing triggers—like sales or the infamous "limited time offer"—is step one in resisting. Next time you're tempted, pause. Take a deep breath and walk away for ten minutes, or even sleep on it overnight. The urge will often pass, and you'll realize you didn't need that item anyway.

Peer pressure can be another nemesis in managing finances. Ever feel like everyone around you is flashing the latest gadgets or hitting up pricey spots? Social influences can make us spend just to fit in, even when it's outside our budget. Set personal financial boundaries by knowing what you're willing to spend on social activities without breaking the bank. Communicating these goals with friends helps, too. Most people respect honesty and might even share similar financial constraints.

FINANCIAL TOOLS AND APPS FOR TEENS

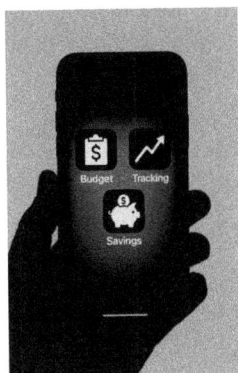

Welcome to the era of digital finance. Financial apps help make handling your cash as easy as sending a snap or recording a TikTok video. These apps become your very own digital assistant that not only tracks what you spend but also helps you save and invest. I wanted to walk you through some of the most popular apps to get you started.

1. **YNAB (You Need A Budget)** & **PocketGuard** are designed to transform budgeting from a chore into a breeze. These apps let you set spending limits, track your expenses, and find out where all your money is going before it vanishes into thin air.
2. Then there's **Acorns** and **Qapital**—your personal savings ninjas. They round up your purchases and stash away the spare change, so you save without even noticing. It's like finding forgotten money in your jeans every time you do laundry, but better.

Technology has revolutionized how we manage money. Gone are the days of scribbling expenses in a notebook or hoarding receipts like some sort of financial packrat. With real-time expense tracking, you can see exactly where your cash flows—faster than you can say "impulse buy." These apps take the guesswork out of saving by automating the process. You can set rules for transferring money to savings every time you get paid or even after every cup of overpriced coffee you buy. This automation not only boosts your bank balance but also enhances your financial literacy without you having to crack open a textbook.

Choosing the right tools can feel a bit like picking out the perfect pair of shoes—you want something that fits just right and matches your style. When selecting financial apps, look for user-friendly interfaces that don't make you feel like you're navigating a spaceship's control panel. Features should align with your goals; if saving for a summer trip is your aim, find an app specializing in setting and tracking savings targets. Some apps offer goal-setting features or even gamify the savings process, turning something mundane into a fun challenge.

But let's not ignore the elephant in the room: security. Ensuring your financial information stays safe with all this data flying around is crucial. Think of strong passwords as the front-line defense against digital pickpockets. Don't be that person who uses "123456" or "password" because it's easy to remember. Instead, get creative with passwords by combining random words and numbers, or better yet, use a password manager to track them all. Two-factor authentication is another layer of security you shouldn't skip—it's like having a security guard at the door who checks ID before letting anyone in.

$$ LEVEL UP MONEY MOVES $$

Use what you have learned in this chapter to

1. ☐ <u>**Begin creating your financial goals**</u>

Grab a notebook or open a notes app on your phone. Write down three things you want to save for by the following year. For each goal, make sure it meets the SMART criteria we talked about earlier. Once you have your goals defined, list out small actions you can take each week to move closer to achieving them. Remember, every super achievement starts with a plan and a first step.

Saving isn't about deprivation; it's about empowerment and foresight. Whether aiming for something tangible like that bike or something more abstract like peace of mind, smart saving is your ticket. So gear up and take action today—your future self will thank you!

2. ☐ Reflect on your Needs vs. Wants

Grab a sheet of paper and jot down ten recent purchases. Label each as a need or a want. Reflect on whether each want was worth its cost or if it was driven by impulse or peer pressure. This exercise will provide insights into spending habits and areas for improvement.

Remember, being smart with money doesn't mean never having fun or enjoying life's luxuries. It's about balance and making informed choices that align with personal values and financial goals. By understanding needs versus wants, prioritizing spending, resisting impulse buys, and managing social pressures, you're setting yourself up for financial stability and empowerment. This isn't just about saving money—it's about creating a life where your choices are intentional and aligned with what truly matters to you.

3. ☐ Select a Financial Tracking app

As you navigate the world of finances, keep in mind that every decision counts towards building the future you envision. Smart spending today means more freedom tomorrow to pursue passions, adventures, and dreams without financial stress holding you back. So go ahead and enjoy life's treats now and then, but do so with mindfulness and purpose, ensuring that each choice supports the bigger picture of your financial well-being.

2

BANK ACCOUNTS 101: CHECKING VS. SAVINGS

Opening a bank account might seem as thrilling as watching paint dry. Still, it's actually a pretty big step towards being financially savvy. Let's kick things off by breaking down the differences between checking and savings accounts. Think of a checking account like a wallet. It's where your money hangs out when you need easy access for everyday spending. Features of checking accounts usually include a debit card, which you can swipe at stores or use to withdraw cash from ATMs. They're all about convenience, making paying for stuff like your Netflix subscription or that midnight pizza craving easy. You can think of them as the social butterflies of the banking world—always out and about.

In contrast, savings accounts are more like a secure, quiet place where your money can chill and grow. They're designed for saving, not spending. Savings accounts typically offer interest, meaning the bank pays you a little extra to keep your money there. It's like a comfy hammock for your cash, where it can relax and multiply over time, perfect for stashing away funds for bigger goals like a car or a college fund. But don't expect the same flexibility as a checking account; savings accounts usually limit the monthly withdrawals you can make.

HOW TO SET UP A BANK ACCOUNT – CHECKING VS. SAVINGS?

First, ask yourself the questions below. Once you have answered all six questions, review the table at the end of this chapter. It will show you the features included in each of these accounts.

1. **Will I need quick access to my money for spending or bills?**

   → If yes, you need a **checking account** (for everyday use like debit cards, bills, and direct deposits).

2. **Am I trying to save money for a future goal (like a car, college, or emergency fund)?**

   → If yes, you need a **savings account** (earns interest and helps resist impulse spending).

3. **Do I want to earn interest on money I don't need right away?**

   → That's what a **savings account** is for.

4. **Will I be getting a paycheck or allowance, and I want to spend it gradually?**

   → A **checking account** is ideal for managing and spending income.

5. **Do I need a debit card to shop or use online subscriptions?**

   → You'll need a **checking account** for that.

6. **Am I ready to build good money habits and track both saving and spending?**

→ Consider opening **both** accounts to organize your money better.

Pro Tip: Most teens benefit from **having both accounts**—use checking for spending and savings for goals.

How do you get started with opening an account?

So, how do you get started with your very own bank account?

1. First things first, gather your documents. You'll need an ID (like a driver's license or passport) and your Social Security Number. Some banks also ask for proof of address. A school report card or school enrollment letter should suffice.
2. Next up, choose where to park your cash. Banks and credit unions both offer accounts, but there are slight differences. Banks are generally larger, with more branches and ATMs, while credit unions often have lower fees and better rates since they're member-owned. Shopping around and finding the best fit for your needs is essential.
3. Once you've selected a bank or credit union, the actual process of opening an account is pretty straightforward. You can often do it online or in person.
4. Fill out an application, provide your documents, and deposit money to get things rolling. And voilà! You're an official account holder.

Now that you've got an account, keeping an eye on what's happening with your money is crucial. Regularly checking your account statements helps you spot any fees, errors, or sneaky subscriptions you forgot about. Online banking tools make this super easy; you can log in anytime to see your balance, track transactions, and even set up alerts for when your funds dip below a certain amount. It's like having a financial watchdog that barks when things go awry.

Banks do more than just hold your money; they offer tools to help manage it effectively. Many banks provide apps and online platforms that let you set financial goals, create budgets, and monitor spending patterns. Some even offer educational resources or access to financial advisors who can guide you on everything from saving for college to planning a vacation on a budget. Make use of these. They are extraordinarily beneficial.

Setting up **account alerts** is another smart move. This is one that I highly recommend. These handy notifications can tell you when your balance is low or when you've been charged a fee. Think of it as having a digital assistant keeping tabs on your finances so you don't have to stress about missing anything important. These alerts can also alert you to fraud. They might text you information about a questionable transaction. Pay close attention and respond promptly when contacted by the bank's fraud department.

Understanding how banks work in the grand scheme of things helps demystify financial management. It turns banking from something that feels like an adult-only club into a powerful ally in achieving your financial dreams. So, while it might not seem all that exciting at first glance, mastering the basics of checking and savings accounts is like unlocking level one in the epic game of life.

Pro Tip: Schedule an in-person visit to open your first bank account. In this way, the banker can take the time to explain all of the cool features and resources available to you.

Side By Side Comparison of Savings Vs. Checking Accounts

Feature	Checking Account	Savings Account
Purpose	Daily Spending & Money Management	Savings goals for emergencies
Access	High (debit card, ATM, online, checks)	Limited (withdrawals may be restricted
Interest Earned	Usually little to no	Yes - earns interest over time
Debit Card	Yes	No (usually)
Best For	Paying bills, shopping, and receiving a paycheck	Building savings, emergency fund
Spending Limitations	No limit (but watch for overdraft!)	May have withdrawal limits per month
Encouages	Convenience and regular transactyions	Savings and financial discipline
Linked To	Can be linked to savings for overdraft protection	Can be linked to checking to automate savings

$$ LEVEL UP MONEY MOVES $$

1. ☐ Determine what kind of **bank account** you need and what features you are looking for
2. ☐ Use your first paycheck or the allowance money you have saved in your sock drawer to open a checking, savings, or both account.

3

MASTERING THE ART OF BUDGETING

Now that you have **categorized your needs vs. wants** and **opened your first bank account**, it is time to **track where your money is going**. This is where we learn how to **budget**. Budgeting isn't about limits—it's about taking control. When you know where your money's going and you've planned ahead for what matters, you gain the freedom to spend with confidence and not worry. It's your money, your plan, your power.

Simply put, a budget is a plan you make for your money. It's like a map that tells your dollars where to go rather than wondering where they went. You track your monthly income, categorize expenses, and set aside cash for savings and investments. Think of it as a game plan for financial victory, where you're the coach calling the shots.

Creating your first budget might sound daunting, but it's easier than you think. Start by listing all your income sources, such as your part-time job, allowance, or even birthday cash from Grandma. Next, identify your expenses. Split them into fixed expenses like monthly subscription fees and variable expenses like snacks and outings with friends. Now, here's the fun part: use a tool to help you visualize this. A simple spreadsheet does wonders, but if you're more tech-savvy, apps like **Mint** provide a user-friendly experience that syncs with your bank account, categorizing transactions automatically (Better Money Habits, n.d.).

Sticking to your budget is where the magic happens. Setting one up is easy, but tough to stick with when temptations arise. However, this discipline pays off when your savings grow, and your goals are within reach. Tracking progress is crucial; apps can send alerts when you're nearing spending limits on certain categories. And if life throws a curveball—like unexpected school trip fees or emergency car repairs—adjust your budget to accommodate these changes without derailing your financial plans.

Regular budget reviews are like check-ins with yourself to ensure you're on track. Set a reminder for a monthly budget review session—a time to assess what worked and what didn't. Maybe you overspent on eating out but saved on transport by carpooling or biking to school. Use these insights to tweak your budget for the upcoming month. This adaptability ensures you're prepared for anything life throws at you, from surprise expenses to changes in income.

Pro Tip: Track your spending at least weekly so you can adjust for changes. Set a reminder and allocate 30 minutes to reviewing all of the week's transactions.

Pro Tip: An app such as **EveryDollar** empowers you to take charge of every expense by requiring you to "approve" each transaction before it can be allocated to a budget category.

BUDGETING FOR FUN: BALANCING ENJOYMENT AND RESPONSIBILITY

Ah, the sweet allure of "fun money"—the delightful pool of cash set aside prominently for the sheer pleasure of indulgence and amusement, entirely free from obligatory chains. Establishing a specific monthly **fun money allowance** is not merely important; it's an art form of financial savvy designed to foster happiness. It's like setting aside some of your money just for your favorite stuff, customized to fit your vibe and goals inside your bigger money plan. Whether it's the joy of sharing bubble tea with the company of cherished friends, savoring each sweet sip, or the digital thrill of downloading the latest game that takes you on an adventure from the comfort of your home, having these funds earmarked solely for enjoyment liberates you to bask in little pleasures without derailing your broader financial plan. It's essential to internalize the philosophy that emphasizes experiences over tangible possessions. Memories, those delightful mental postcards of joyful moments, endure far beyond the ephemeral excitement of a new gadget poised to become a dust collector.

Mastering the delicate dance of balancing needs versus wants forms the bedrock of sage, responsible budgeting. Envision dedicating a defined percentage of your monthly income exclusively to entertaining activities. It's like making a confident, declarative statement, "Yes, I'm going to savor life's manifold joys, yet remain vigilant over my fiscal stability." The intricate art of planning occasional splurges—whether it's gifting oneself a magical live concert experience or orchestrating a blissful weekend getaway—is imbued with ease when you've prudently earmarked a segment of your budget solely for these enchanting moments. It's the perfect dance of enjoying life presently with the wisdom not to compromise your financial safety net for the future.

CREATIVE BUDGETING IDEAS

For those who relish thinking outside the box, exploring alternative budgeting techniques might fit the bill. The ingeniously straightforward "No Spend" challenge is precisely what it sounds like—embark on a period of spending nothing (or as little as possible) to reassess and realign your spending habits. It's like hitting the reset button on your budget, enlightening you on how much you can save by refraining from indulging in every impulse purchase.

Bartering and trading goods or services inject an old-school charm into modern financial practices. Engage in skill exchange with friends or community members—perhaps trade tutoring for guitar lessons or arrange a clothes swap with a buddy instead of buying new ones. It's like infusing a retro flair into your finances and witnessing how far creativity can propel you.

These hacks go beyond mere monetary savings—they instill a sense of self-reliance and resourcefulness, transforming budgeting into an invigorating challenge rather than a dreaded chore. Armed with these innovative strategies in your toolkit, you're not just managing money but mastering the art of being financially astute, maintaining an ever-present sense of fun and engagement. Who knew the path to financial savvy could be so rewarding?

OVERCOMING BUDGET BLUNDERS: ADJUSTING AND ADAPTING

Now that you've painstakingly crafted a budget with meticulous attention to detail, feeling like a financial wizard on the brink of conquering all monetary challenges, only to discover a week later that you've underestimated how much those seemingly harmless daily smoothies are costing you. Oops indeed! Underestimating expenses is one of the sneakiest and most elusive mistakes out there. Another common mistake is not accounting for irregular expenses, such as birthday gifts for friends, spontaneous outings, or emergency purchases that pop up when you least expect them. These seemingly small blunders can accumulate over time, stealthily undermining your financial plan and throwing it into complete disarray.

But don't panic! Remember, fixing budget missteps isn't as insurmountable a task as it might initially seem. The first and perhaps most essential step is to take a deep breath, acknowledge the blunder calmly, and then diligently get down to business. Reallocating funds from discretionary spheres to more essential categories can truly be a lifesaver in such circumstances. Perhaps it means opting out of that extra takeout night this week, an indulgence you enjoy but can temporarily sacrifice, and redirecting those funds toward covering your unexpected expenses. Setting aside a buffer for unforeseen costs is a crucial strategy as well. Think of it as a safety net, a little financial cushion that softens the blow when life unpredictably throws you a curveball.

Now, let's delve into the importance of flexibility within budgeting. Budgets aren't rigid, unyielding structures etched in stone; they should be more like a flexible rubber band—stretchy, adjustable, and accommodating. Life is continually evolving, and so should your budget. If your income fluctuates, such as with the unpredictable hours of a part-time job, you'll want your budget to be adaptable and roll with those changes. By incorporating a flexible spending category, you provide the necessary leeway to handle those unforeseen expenses without completely derailing your financial plan. Consider it a backup plan for your backup plan, offering a sense of security and readiness for whatever financial challenges may arise.

Mistakes aren't failures but invaluable stepping stones towards gaining financial wisdom. When you stumble, use that moment as an opportunity to reflect thoughtfully on your spending decisions. Maybe that impulse purchase wasn't as fulfilling or necessary as it first seemed, or perhaps you've unearthed a hidden cost that was previously overlooked. Implementing new strategies for improvement turns these blunders into valuable learning experiences. Developing better habits might mean setting clearer priorities or utilizing helpful financial tools and apps to keep a closer track of your spending patterns and tendencies.

$$ LEVEL UP MONEY MOVES $$

1. ☐ Interactive Element: App Scavenger Hunt - Find a budgeting app that suits your preferences

Take a moment to explore the app store on your phone. Search for some budgeting apps that catch your eye. Download them and spend about 15 minutes navigating their features. Do they offer what you need? Are they easy to use? Note down what you liked and disliked about each app. This exercise will help you determine which tools best fit your financial style.

Security concerns aside, these apps are more than just digital piggy banks; they're educational tools that help build financial habits and knowledge. Whether automating savings or offering insights into spending patterns, they empower you to take charge of your finances without sitting through a boring economics class. Plus, many of these tools provide tips and tricks to help you along the way, kind of like having a financial coach in your pocket.

And remember, while technology makes managing money easier, it also requires vigilance. Be aware of potential scams or phishing attempts that could compromise your information. Always download apps from reputable sources and read reviews to ensure they're trustworthy. Stay updated on best security practices because knowledge is power when protecting your financial data.

In this fast-paced digital age, mastering financial tools is like learning to ride a bike—once you get the hang of it, you'll wonder how you ever managed without them. By integrating these technologies into your financial routine, you're not just keeping up with the times; you're setting yourself up for success in a world where money management skills are as crucial as knowing how to swipe left or right on Tinder.

Budgeting App Comparison 2025

App Name	Budgeting Style	Free Version	Bank Sync	Auto Categorization	Notable Features
YNAB	Zero-based	✕	☑	☑	Goal tracking, rollover budgeting, workshops
EveryDollar	Zero-based	☑ (basic)	☑ (premium)	☑	Simple interface, bill tracking
Goodbudget	Envelope-based	☑	✕	✕	Manual entry, sync across devices
PocketGuard	Simplified zero-based	☑	☑	☑	"In My Pocket" feature, debt payoff plans
Simplifi	Goal-based	✕	☑	☑	Cash flow projections, spending plans
Empower	Investment-focused	☑	☑	☑	Net worth tracking, retirement planning
Monarch	Collaborative	✕	☑	☑	Advisor access, household sharing
Rocket Money	Subscription management	☑	☑	☑	Bill negotiation, credit monitoring
Honeydue	Couples budgeting	☑	☑	☑	Shared budgets, bill reminders, chat feature

Table 1: Budgeting App Comparison

2. ☐ **Exercise: Budgeting Reality Check**

Track every penny you earn and spend for one month. Use a notebook or an app; it doesn't matter as long as you do it consistently. Review your spending habits at the end of the month. Where did most of your money go? Be honest—did you really need that third iced coffee last week? This exercise provides valuable insight into your financial habits and helps identify areas for improvement.

Budgeting isn't about restricting yourself; it's about freeing yourself from financial worry. Once you've got the hang of it, you'll find that budgeting becomes second nature, like brushing your teeth or scrolling through social media. It's not about saying no to fun; it's about planning for the fun things today so you won't stress about them when it comes time to pay for them. Think about it this way. You have been eyeing that new gaming system or wanting to take that trip with your friends. Budgeting allows you to buy the gaming system or take that trip. It might take a few months, but with a budget, it lets you know exactly how much you will need to save over what period, turning these dreams into reality.

The beauty of budgeting lies in its flexibility; no two budgets are identical because no two lives are identical. Your budget should reflect your priorities and lifestyle, adapting as you grow and your circumstances change. Remember, a budget isn't set in stone; it's a living document that evolves with you. Whether saving for college or planning a summer road trip with friends, budgeting lays the foundation for achieving these milestones without financial strain or anxiety.

Budgeting is about empowerment—taking control of your financial future and making informed choices that align with your dreams and values. It's about being proactive rather than reactive, ensuring that money serves you rather than vice versa. As you create and refine your budget, remember that every dollar has potential; it's up to you to decide how best to use it. So grab that calculator, open that spreadsheet or budget app, and start building a budget that works for you today!

Option 1: Digital Budgeting - Using Apps to Stay on Track

In today's vibrant and fast-paced tech-driven world, harnessing the power of budgeting apps is akin to having a diligent and highly efficient mini financial advisor nestled right in the palm of your hand or snugly tucked in your pocket. These ingenious digital tools are designed to bring simplicity and clarity to the complex web of personal finance management by seamlessly automating the arduous task of expense tracking and presenting real-time updates with pristine accuracy. Picture receiving instantaneous notifications when you decide to make a purchase, gently nudging you to remain aware of your financial standing, and alerting you to how much leeway you have left in your monthly spending allowance. Not only do these apps effortlessly and automatically sort and categorize your expenditures, but they also provide a comprehensive snapshot of where your precious dollars and cents are flowing, without you having to lift a solitary finger. It's much like having a meticulous and tireless personal assistant who thrives on crunching numbers around the clock. Additionally, these real-time budget updates ensure you are perpetually informed, providing you with the empowerment needed to make astute and informed financial decisions on the go.

When selecting the ideal budgeting app, the process can feel as nuanced and important as choosing the perfect playlist for an unforgettable road trip—it requires the right mix of features and aesthetics that effortlessly align to keep everything running smoothly. You should opt for an application boasting an easy-to-use, ergonomic interface that doesn't demand a doctoral degree to navigate. More intuitive than intimidating, the ideal app aligns harmoniously with your unique and personal financial needs. Consider the key features that resonate with your objectives. Are you engaging in strategic saving for an extravagant vacation or perhaps diligently tracking your journey out of debt? Furthermore, examine whether the app maintains compatibility with your specific bank or financial institutions to ensure seamless transaction synchronization without complications. When you find a good match, it translates to less time spent tinkering with complex settings and more focus on actively managing and optimizing your financial portfolio. Apps, when skillfully integrated with your financial aspirations, can be revolutionary. Many platforms now possess the capability to allow you to set customized savings goals directly within their seamless digital environments, gently reminding you of your progression with each incremental step forward. Whether your objective is to wisely save for the latest tech gadget, a luxurious designer item, or pay off that nagging credit card debt, these visually engaging goal structures hold you accountable. It's akin to having a personalized digital cheerleader who enthusiastically encourages you each time you bravely resist succumbing to the temptation of unnecessary indulgences or expenditures on trifling gadgets and snacks.

In the realm of digital budgeting, security is paramount. No one desires their sensitive financial information to be floating in the limitless expanse of cyberspace, akin to loose coins carelessly dropped in the crevices of a couch. Ensuring the app you're considering employs robust data encryption methods to safeguard your vital information is crucial. Dive into privacy settings and reviews meticulously to ascertain that the app isn't in the habit of sharing your cherished data with untrustworthy third parties. Adhering to best practices, such as crafting strong, unique passwords and enabling two-factor authentication, adds an indispensable layer of protection—a digital bouncer standing firm at the entrance to the exclusive VIP section of your personal financial club.

Option 2: The Envelope System - A Hands-On Cash Approach

The envelope system is a straightforward and practical budgeting method that is simple to navigate. The core idea revolves around allocating real, tangible cash into distinct envelopes, each labeled for different spending categories—think groceries, entertainment, or perhaps that peculiar hobby you decided to delve into last summer. When the cash in a designated envelope is depleted, that signals the end of spending in that category for the month. It's akin to having a strict yet loving financial guardian or mentor who discourages frivolous splurges on unnecessary app downloads or other fleeting temptations.

Getting started with the envelope system can initially feel akin to setting up your own miniature banking institution at home. First and foremost, it requires you to pinpoint your distinct budget categories. Consider every realm of expenditure where you habitually part with money—be it food, leisure activities, savings, or a bit set aside for those unforeseen emergencies life occasionally throws your way. Once you've meticulously identified these categories, the next step is to thoughtfully determine how much cash should be allocated to each one, a process demanding introspection and a realistic evaluation of your necessities. Be careful not to leave yourself subsisting on instant noodles for an entire week simply because you got a bit carried away when purchasing concert tickets. With your categories and amounts firmly decided, withdraw the total sum from your bank at the start of the month, placing the designated amounts into each envelope. Well done! You've now established a tangible budget – a financial plan you can physically hold in your hands and easily track.

The beauty of the envelope system lies in the undeniable truth of physically watching your money dwindle away. Witnessing cash disappear between your fingers holds a power unlike that of swiping a card, often making spending decisions weigh more heavily on the conscience. It's like a visual guilt trip—one wielded for your financial benefit this time. Handling cash can significantly diminish the allure of overspending, as you cannot effortlessly swipe away your savings as one might with the quick slide of a card. When it's gone, it's genuinely gone, compelling you to adhere to your budget with the same tenacity as gum fuses to a hot sidewalk.

But hey, we fully understand. Not everyone is inclined to wander the world with envelopes brimming with cash like it's a relic of the 1980s. We inhabit a digital age where electronic payments have swiftly soared to supremacy. Fear not! The envelope system, flexible and enduring, has adapted to modernity, manifesting in apps like Goodbudget, which allow the creation of virtual envelopes for each spending category. These apps closely emulate the traditional physical system but bring the added convenience of residing within your smartphone. Allowing you to track your spending in real-time without the fuss of physically carrying around paper envelopes, you can feel like a financial virtuoso with every tap on your screen.

An alternative for those who prefer the swipe of plastic over paper is the utilization of debit cards designed with spending limits, effectively mimicking the envelope method in a digital format. Certain banks now offer accounts where it's feasible to establish spending limits per category each month—a contemporary twist on a timeless classic, merging the disciplined essence of cash handling with the effortless nature of electronic transactions. This approach captures all the benefits of strict spending limits without accompanying envelopes, proving perfect for the tech-savvy budget enthusiast.

In essence, the envelope system—grounded in traditional paper or innovatively digital—centers around establishing boundaries for your spending habits. It fosters a mindfulness that prompts reflection before purchasing, ensuring that what truly matters takes precedence in your financial dealings. Whether opting for physical cash or a digital application, implementing these finite limits encourages healthier financial habits and effectively curtails unwarranted splurging. The true elegance of this system lies within its inherent flexibility; it's adaptable to seamlessly integrate into diverse lifestyle dynamics. Doing so lets you watch as your financial stress recedes into the background, replaced by an empowering sense of control and newfound savings.

3. ☐ Track your expenses

Track for an entire month, with weekly check-ins. Use a notebook, an Excel spreadsheet, Google Sheets, or an app. Whatever makes sense for you.

4. ☐ Reflection Section: Learning from Budget Blunders

Grab a journal or your favorite notepad. Allow yourself the time and space to reflect earnestly on a recent budgeting mistake you made. What exactly went wrong, and in what way did it affect your overall financial plan? Now, contemplate what you could do differently next time to avoid making similar mistakes. Write down at least two strategies you can implement moving forward, devising a plan that resonates with your financial goals.

Remember, budgeting isn't about achieving perfection; it's about making consistent progress and cultivating adaptability to changing circumstances. Every blunder you encounter is an opportunity to learn something new and refine your approach. The more you engage in this practice, the better you become at anticipating challenges and navigating them gracefully. These experiences incrementally shape and fortify your financial savvy, better preparing you for more significant financial decisions and challenges down the road.

As you navigate the intricate world of budgeting, remind yourself that it's perfectly okay to make mistakes—everyone does! What truly matters is how you choose to respond to these missteps and what valuable lessons you extract from them. Embrace the process wholeheartedly, maintain your flexibility, and offer yourself the grace to adjust your course as needed. Budgeting is not just a financial undertaking; it's an ongoing adventure filled with twists, turns, and precious lessons to be garnered along the way.

4

TRACKING YOUR SPENDING: WHERE DOES YOUR MONEY GO?

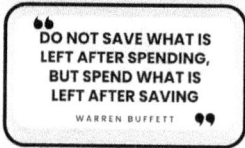

Welcome to the art of tracking spending, where we unravel the mysteries of where your cash disappears. Identifying spending patterns is crucial. Ever notice how some weeks you're a money-saving superstar and others you're splurging like there's no tomorrow? Recognizing these patterns can help you budget better. And pinpointing unnecessary expenses? That's like finding hidden treasure. You'll be surprised how much you can save when you cut out impulse buys or those subscriptions you forgot about three months ago.

> **DO NOT SAVE WHAT IS LEFT AFTER SPENDING, BUT SPEND WHAT IS LEFT AFTER SAVING**
>
> WARREN BUFFETT

Now, how do you actually track this spending? For some, a trusty **notebook or note app** works wonders. Jot down every single thing you buy, from the morning latte to the late-night pizza. It's tedious but surprisingly effective. Alternatively, **spreadsheets** can be your digital best friend. Log your expenses in neat columns and watch as your spending habits unfold before your eyes. If you're more of an app enthusiast, there's something for you too. Apps like **Expensify** make tracking expenses a breeze. They categorize your spending automatically and even generate snazzy reports. Alternatively, you can use your debit card for everything, and you can **track every expense using your banking app**. They typically have features that automatically categorize your expenses.

Speaking of categories, let's break down expenses into fixed versus variable ones. **Fixed expenses** are like that one friend who always shows up uninvited—rent, phone bills, subscriptions, etc. They are those bills that come knocking every month. **Variable expenses** are a bit more unpredictable, like weekend adventures or random shopping sprees. Then, there's **essential** versus **discretionary** spending. Essentials are the boring but necessary things—think food, phone, and transport. Discretionary spending is where you get to have fun—movies, concerts, and that limited-edition hoodie.

> *Pro tip*: Even when an expense is fixed (e.g., an app subscription), it can fall into the discretionary expenses category. Take a close look at ALL expenses, fixed and variable, to determine if any can be eliminated.

Regular expense reviews are your secret weapon in budgeting. Think of them as monthly check-ins with yourself to see how you're doing financially. Reviewing your spending each month can reveal opportunities for savings, like realizing you spent way too much on delivery food when cooking would've been cheaper and healthier (but let's be honest, who doesn't love a good pizza night?). These reviews help you make informed budget adjustments. Maybe it's cutting back on those daily coffees or putting more into savings for that dream vacation.

Think of stretching your dollars like a challenging yet rewarding game, where the prize is the satisfaction of extra money left over at the end of the month. Start with couponing and discount codes, powerful allies in this financial quest. It might sound like a habit reserved for your grandma's generation, but discovering unexpected savings can be exhilarating. Apps and browser extensions such as **Honey** and **RetailMeNot** act like digital sleuths, tirelessly scouring the vast recesses of the internet to uncover hidden discounts so you don't have to. In essence, it's as if you have a devoted personal shopper whose sole mission is to save you hard-earned cash. Moreover, when you're shopping in brick-and-mortar stores, remember the importance of asking about any available discounts or sales. Surprisingly, simply inquiring can uncover a sweet deal you might have otherwise overlooked.

Buying in bulk can drastically stretch your budget further, akin to a clever magic trick: acquiring more items while expending less cash. Consider securing a membership at a bulk store; you'll soon find yourself basking in a sea of savings. Stock up on fundamental necessities like snacks or toiletries, and you'll pat yourself on the back later when you avoid those impromptu, expensive runs to the store. Not to mention, with a well-stocked pantry, you'll be the hero at study group sessions, always ready to provide sustenance for hungry friends.

DIY projects and repairs emerge as your budget's steadfast allies. By fixing things yourself, you not only save a considerable chunk of money but also cultivate a genuine sense of accomplishment. As your virtual DIY guru, YouTube offers tutorials for everything from meticulously sewing a missing button to intricately building a bookshelf. Why pay someone to perform a task that you can master in an afternoon? Plus, the joy of narrating a triumphant DIY success story becomes an added bonus to relish.

Pro Tip: Mastered the DIY project? Now you've got a skill you can use to earn money—maybe even start your own mini-business!

SMART SHOPPING TECHNIQUES

Smart shopping isn't solely about deciding what to buy; it concerns how and when to execute those purchases. **Comparison shopping** serves as a transformative game-changer in this endeavor. Before hitting that enticing "buy now" button, take a moment to browse multiple sites, ensuring you're securing the best possible price. Few things feel worse than purchasing an item only to discover it was available cheaper elsewhere. Additionally, timing your purchases strategically can lead to significant savings. Wait patiently for sales, shop during off-peak seasons, or employ cashback apps to efficiently maximize every dollar spent.

Negotiation transcends the realm of business deals; it seamlessly fits into everyday life, too. **Asking for student discounts** can deftly trim serious bucks off your expenses. Always keep that student ID handy— it acts like a golden ticket to uncover numerous savings opportunities. Moreover, don't hesitate to **negotiate subscription fees**. Whether it's your trusty streaming service or gym membership, a simple phone call and a polite request for a better rate can achieve surprisingly favorable results.

SIGNIFICANCE OF BUDGETED TREATS

Let's turn the spotlight onto the concept of budgeted treats, those delightful mini-celebrations sprinkled along the path of diligent budget adherence. Perhaps you've reached a noteworthy savings mile-stone or maintained your spending discipline for three consecutive months. Why not grace this occasion with a small, well-deserved treat? It could manifest as something as delightful as indulging in a favorite ice cream outing or acquiring that outfit that has been calling for you for months on end. Deliberately planning for special occasions such as birthdays or anniversaries ensures that such moments are marked with indulgence without any shadow of guilt.

Exploring a spectrum of cost-effective entertainment choices can pepper your calendar with enjoyable activities that don't deplete your resources. Scour for free community events swirling around you—consider outdoor concerts that radiate with musical joy, art exhibitions showcasing creativity, or vibrant festivals where culture and fun collide. Such events provide not just entertainment but often present opportunities to savor free samples of delectable food—a delicious double win! Engaging in low-cost hobbies such as hiking through nature's serene landscapes, biking through scenic routes, or joining a local sports league introduces a trove of fun-filled hours without exerting financial pressure. Even something as simple yet profoundly fun as hosting a game night with friends—from board games that test wits to video games that ignite your competitive spirit—can create cherished memories at minimal cost.

MANAGING DIGITAL PAYMENTS: CASHLESS TRANSACTIONS

Imagine a world where cash is as outdated as flip phones and dial-up internet. Welcome to the cashless age, where digital payments reign supreme. We're talking about the likes of Venmo and PayPal, where your money zips from one account to another faster than you can say "I forgot my wallet." And let's not forget contactless payments with smartphones—just a tap and you're out the door with your latte, no fumbling for change required. It's like living in the future, except it's happening right now. Cashless transactions have become the norm, making financial exchanges more convenient than ever.

But how do you actually set up these digital payment methods without feeling like you're hacking into a secret vault? Fear not, it's simpler than you'd think. Start by downloading your app of choice—whether it's Venmo, PayPal, or Apple Pay—and follow their prompts. You'll need to link your bank account or credit card to the app, which is as easy as entering your financial details and verifying your identity. Most apps will walk you through this process, ensuring your info is secure. Then, secure your account like Fort Knox by setting up a strong password. Enable two-factor authentication for an extra layer of defense against the cyber baddies lurking out there.

Once you're set up, the benefits of going cashless are pretty undeniable. Imagine splitting a dinner bill with friends without having to calculate who owes what down to the last penny. Digital payments make it possible with a simple click or swipe. It's convenience at its finest, saving you time and awkward math moments at the table. Plus, tracking expenses becomes a breeze when every transaction is logged in an app. No more guessing where all those $5 bills went—it's all right there on your phone, organized and ready for review like a real-time financial diary.

Of course, with great power comes great responsibility—especially when it comes to keeping your digital transactions safe from prying eyes. Start by avoiding public Wi-Fi like it's the plague when making transactions. Those networks are like open doors for hackers looking to siphon your hard-earned money. Instead, stick to secure networks or use your mobile data for peace of mind. Remember that two-factor authentication we mentioned? It's not just for show. It adds an extra step in verifying your identity when you log in, making it harder for anyone else to access your account.

In this digital age, managing payments without cash isn't just convenient—it's practically expected. From buying concert tickets to paying back your friend for last week's pizza run, digital payments have made life smoother and faster. They're like having a financial assistant in your pocket, ready to handle transactions with ease and efficiency. But remember, while enjoying this convenience, always stay vigilant about security. With these tools at your fingertips and smart practices in place, you'll navigate the cashless world like a pro, avoiding pitfalls and keeping your finances secure in the process.

As we draw to a close on our insightful exploration of the dynamic world of Budgeting, remember that these versatile tools are designed not just to simplify but to enhance how you handle your finances efficiently. By adeptly leveraging and harnessing their multifaceted features, you can achieve a harmonious alignment of your spending with your broader financial objectives, track your progress with real-time accuracy, and safeguard your personal information with due diligence. Looking forward, we shall delve into strategic saving techniques that empower you to build a solid financial future without necessitating the compromise of the enjoyment and vibrancy of your current lifestyle. So, prepare yourself to embark on this exciting journey of learning how to expand your savings without ever needing to sacrifice the fun and enjoyment life has to offer!

$$ LEVEL UP MONEY MOVES $$

1. ☐ Reflect on your tracked expenses

In the previous chapter, you tracked your expenses for one week. Now, reflect on what they were, adding them to your budget. For example: you might have missed an app subscription or two. Make a note of areas where you think you might have overspent. At the end of the week, categorize each expense and reflect on what surprised you. Was it the daily coffee runs or that one Saturday night out? This exercise will give you insight into your spending habits and highlight areas for improvement.

Tracking expenses may sound like a chore at first, but it's the foundation of mastering budgeting. It empowers you to take control of your finances and make choices that align with your goals. So grab that notebook or download an app, and start tracking where your money goes. You'll be amazed at what you discover—and how much more in control of your financial destiny you'll feel!

2. ☐ Cancel any discretionary expenses, such as app subscriptions, to save a little money.

3. ☐ Track your fun money.

Be diligent and track how much you spend every day for one month. At the end of the month, you should better understand how much fun money you want to allocate each month.

Set forth a fun money budget for the month and meticulously track your spending journeys with this fund. Upon the culmination of the month, take a reflective walk through memory lane of your experiences and assess which escapades were indeed worth the spend and which may have fallen short of expectations. This insightful exercise aids in fine-tuning what sincerely brings joy while remaining mindful not to overspend.

The essence of fun money isn't about liberating financial caution to the whims of the wind; it's a delicate art of weaving bursts of joy into the fabric of responsibly curated budget management. By carefully allotting explicit funds for enjoyment and harmonizing this with life's necessities, you cultivate an equilibrium with money that facilitates both steadfast stability and spontaneous delights. As you navigate these intricate waters, remember that the ultimate success lies in striking an optimal balance between accountability and indulgence. Ensuring that as you revel in today's pleasures, you are simultaneously nurturing a secure financial foundation for the dreams of tomorrow.

4. ☐ **Update next month's budget allocations** based on last month's tracking of expenses and fun money.

5

SAVING FOR SHORT AND LONG-TERM GOALS

EMERGENCY FUNDS: YOUR FINANCIAL SAFETY NET

The music's up, the vibe's chill, and the sunset's hitting just right—then suddenly your car lets out a noise that could score a horror film. Not exactly the plot twist you wanted. Or maybe you're feeling under the weather, and a cold leads to the sniffles that require a more thorough doctor's visit. These are precisely the moments when an emergency fund becomes your best friend. An emergency fund is like that guardian angel you didn't realize you urgently needed until life throws an unexpected plot twist your way. It's a specific stash of cash set aside just for those unforeseen expenses, like the surprise car repairs, unforeseen medical bills, or a cracked phone screen that pop up when you least anticipate them. Having this financial cushion provides peace of mind, offering reassurance and stability as it helps you stay afloat without having to engage in the dreaded call-for-cash dance with family or friends or spiral into tenser financial strategies.

But how do you cultivate this magical emergency fund? The journey begins with setting a realistic target—perhaps a modest amount like $500. It's sufficient to tackle minor mishaps, which eases the overwhelming burden often associated with financial surprises. Think of it as nurturing a fledgling tree; it needs a strong foundation to grow. Once you've hit those initial savings goals, aim higher. Gradually increase your savings over time through a budgeted, automated savings amount (e.g., $100/month for 5 months).

> *Pro Tip:* Utilize a savings account to maintain its separation from your everyday spending. Think of it as a sacred vault, the financial vault, that only gets cracked open for actual emergencies, not for that enticing new game release or the alluring concert tickets, which may regularly beckon you.

Now that you have an emergency fund, let's answer the question: What precisely qualifies as an emergency? An emergency isn't simply anything unexpected; it's something that directly affects your well-being or safety irrevocably. Consider medical emergencies, essential car fixes, such as those critical brakes that suddenly stop working, or needing a new battery for your phone. It's definitely not for impulse buys or last-minute road trips with friends. Once you've dipped into your fund, make it the utmost priority to replenish it as quickly as possible. Rebuilding it ensures you're perpetually ready for whatever life throws your way next, enabling you to face it all with confidence.

You might be asking, why even bother with an emergency fund at all? With an emergency fund, you can face unexpected expenses with confidence rather than fear and anxiety. That's the transformative power of an emergency fund. Consider Jamie, for example. She saved diligently over time, and when her laptop suddenly died right before crucial exams, she could replace it without panicking or additional stress. Or think about Alex, who avoided borrowing money from friends or family members when his car needed a new battery replacement, all thanks to his emergency fund. These funds effortlessly transcend beyond mere money; they symbolize the embodiment of maintaining financial independence, fiscal responsibility, and not having to rely on handouts from others unexpectedly during times of need.

COLLEGE SAVINGS: PREPARING FOR HIGHER EDUCATION COSTS

Let's talk about college savings, a topic that might seem to belong to the grown-ups, but trust me, this is your show too. Remember, this is your plan, and like most college-bound students, you will be responsible for paying for a portion, if not all. So, if you have college goals, start saving now. There are quite a few great college saving mechanisms that you could consider. First up, the **529 college savings plan**. You can set up automatic transfers from your checking or savings account into this account, which grows like an investment fund. The difference is that it grows tax-free. Once you are ready to use it, you can withdraw the funds tax-free. More about this in Chapter 8 when we dive into the details of taxes. Most importantly, parents, guardians, and any loved ones in your tribe can contribute. Then there's the **Coverdell Education Savings Account**. This one's a bit similar but with a twist—it's not just for college; you can use it for K-12 expenses too. The contribution limits are smaller, but hey, every bit helps, right? And if you're playing it simple, a regular savings account dedicated to education works too. It's less fancy but gets the job done.

Starting early with college savings is key to gaining financial independence and transitioning into adulthood debt-free. **Compound interest*** is your best buddy here. It's like a small snowball rolling down a hill, picking up more snow (or cash) as time passes. The earlier you start, the bigger it gets by the time you need it. Plus, early saving means less student loan debt to worry about later. What if you could graduate from college without the burden of loans hanging over your

---

* Compound Interest is the money you earn not just on your original amount (called the **principal**)—but also on the **interest that builds up over time**. So you're basically earning **interest on your interest**.

head? It's not just about saving money—it's about buying freedom from future financial stress.

Estimating college costs is like budgeting for a road trip; you need to account for everything from gas to snacks. Start with tuition and fees—those are the biggies. Then add books and supplies; they might seem small, but they can sneak up on you like a ninja in the night. Don't forget about living expenses if you plan to live on campus or even rent an apartment off-campus. But wait, there's help on the horizon! Scholarships and financial aid can ease the burden like a trusty sidekick. Research potential scholarships early and understand how financial aid works to maximize what you can get.

Let's sprinkle in some inspiration with stories of students who saved diligently for their education. Take Mia, for instance. She started working part-time during high school and saved diligently into her 529 plan with help from her parents. By the time she headed to college, her savings covered most of her tuition. Or consider Jake, whose community pooled resources to support local students through a scholarship fund. He combined this with his savings and managed to graduate debt-free. These stories aren't fairy tales—they're achievable with planning and determination.

SETTING REALISTIC FINANCIAL GOALS: SHORT-TERM VS. LONG-TERM

Imagine you're setting out on a cross-country road trip without a map or GPS. Sounds a bit chaotic, right? That's precisely what it's like to manage your finances without a definitive set of financial goals. Without having well-defined financial goals in place, you're essentially just cruising along without any clear direction, hoping you'll end up somewhere positive and financially sound. Goal setting in saving is akin to laying railroad tracks before a train ride—it provides essential direction and a sense of purpose. It offers a way to measure progress, allowing you to determine when you've reached a milestone or when it might be prudent to adjust your course. Plus, there's truly nothing quite like the immense satisfaction of ticking off a box for a goal that has been achieved.

Now, let's delve into the process of differentiating between short-term and long-term goals. Think of short-term goals as the necessary pit stops on your journey—those goals that are achievable within a span of a year, like saving for a new phone, a summer camp, or perhaps a small emergency fund. These are the quick wins that keep you motivated along your journey, sustaining your drive. On the other hand, long-term goals are like preparing for the grand finale, such as saving for college tuition, purchasing your first car, or even putting aside funds for a down payment on a house. These require several years of planning and commitment, and are more akin to marathons than the quick sprints that short-term goals can be. Understanding how to categorize these goals aids in effective strategizing and resource allocation, ensuring that you're able to distribute your resources prudently and focus on what truly matters at any given time.

But how do you actually go about setting goals that won't prematurely find themselves in the graveyard of good intentions? Enter the **SMART criteria**: goals should be **Specific** (clear and precise with no ambiguity), **Measurable** (allowing for progress tracking to see incremental advancements), **Achievable** (realistic given your current resources and limitations), **Relevant** (significant and vital to you and your overarching life plans), and **Time-bound** (establishing a clear deadline for completion). For example, instead of vaguely proclaiming, "I want to save money," a more structured approach would be saying, *"I will save $200 for a new bike by next summer."* Such specificity helps in ensuring clarity and purpose. Prioritizing is also a crucial aspect; not all goals are created equal in terms of weight and priority. Sorting them based on importance and urgency helps to decide where you should focus your energy first and which goals can temporarily take a backseat.

Life can indeed be unpredictable and full of surprises, which is why flexibility plays such a significant role in goal setting. Your goals aren't meant to be set in stone—they're more like malleable clay, ready to be molded as circumstances in your life change. Perhaps you experience an unexpected financial windfall or face an unforeseen expense that derails your plans. Reassessing goals periodically ensures they remain relevant and aligned with your evolving financial situation and priorities. Adapting goals doesn't signify admitting defeat; rather, it's about staying nimble and responsive to life's many twists and turns, ensuring you're perpetually on a path of financial success.

Adaptability Example: You've set a goal to save for a laptop within six months, diligently putting aside the necessary funds. But then, to your surprise and delight, your favorite band announces a world tour with a stop in your town. Suddenly, priorities shift naturally. That's okay! Re-evaluate your timeline or adjust your contributions temporarily. It's about finding a balanced approach and keeping your financial ship steady amidst the inevitable waves.

In this intricate dance of setting and achieving financial goals, remember that each step forward is a notable victory, regardless of the size of that step. You may stumble upon obstacles or need to recalibrate along your journey—the key is **persistence** paired with **adaptability.** Celebrate the victories, however small they may be, learn from any hiccups encountered along the way, and keep progressing forward with your eyes focused firmly on the prize. Each triumph, whether it's a small financial victory or a significant milestone achieved, adds up to success in the grand scheme of your financial journey.

THE POWER OF COMPOUND INTEREST: GROWING YOUR SAVINGS

Compound interest, often likened to a financial superhero quietly blessing your money, is integral to wealth accumulation strategies. Unlike its counterpart, simple interest, which is calculated solely on the original principal amount, compound interest operates on the principal sum and the previously earned interest. To provide an apt analogy, envision a snowball rolling majestically down a hill. With each rotation, it gathers more snow, increasing not only in size but also in speed. This is the quintessence of compound interest—a phenomenon of exponential growth where the pace quickens appreciably as time elapses. By commencing with a seemingly modest sum and permitting it the latitude of time, you can witness your money expand substantially, akin to a seed blossoming into a sprawling tree, laden with fruit.

Simple Interest versus Compound Interest

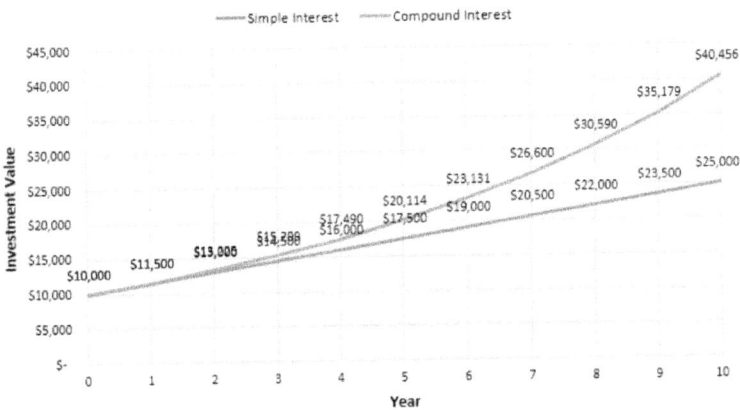

To appreciate the wonders of compound interest, let us examine a tangible scenario.

- **Scenario 1:** You initiate saving **$50 monthly** at the tender **age of 15** with an account offering a 5% annual compounded interest rate. By the time you reach the age of 65, you will have amasse approximately **$80,000.**
- **Scenario 2:** You delay initiation of savings until **age 25** with the same parameters; only then, your total balloons to a mere **$42,000** by 65.

There's a reason starting early is touted as the secret sauce; it's akin to obtaining an exclusive backstage pass to the grand symphony of wealth. This illustration precisely underscores the power and impact of early savings initiation; it's not a cliché but a critical financial strategy.

Now, how can you truly wield compound interest to your advantage? The foremost technique is to initiate savings as soon as practicable. Even if you are able to start with what feels like a meager contribution, every dollar is vital in contributing to this awe-inspiring snowball effect. Additionally, opting for financial institutions offering superior interest rates can significantly enhance your returns. Online banks, frequently characterized by reduced overhead costs, often present more competitive rates than their traditional counterparts, thereby warranting careful consideration. Additionally, focus on accounts that compound interest more frequently—be it monthly or daily—as the more frequent the compounding, the more the money grows. This is comparable to selecting a thrilling roller coaster with additional loops and twirls, which is scary yet leads to an exhilarating payoff.

Embracing a mindset of patience transforms into your hidden weapon in this arena. The singular strength of compound interest lies in its temporal growth capability, necessitating a long-term savings outlook. Design savings goals with a horizon spanning decades, not just mere years, ensuring foresight that your future self will undoubtedly commend. While you might not currently dwell on acquiring luxury vehicles or coordinating lavish vacations, the provisionally postponed gratification is less about sacrifice and more about instituting a financially secure future replete with unrestricted choice and diminished anxieties.

Structuring long-term savings objectives also serves as a navigational compass. Envision not only the sum you wish to accumulate but what said financial milestone enables you to fulfill—a comfortable home-ownership, pioneering a business dream, or traversing the globe. These aspirations are the bedrock of a structured savings strategy. Maintaining your commitment is pivotal; life is adept at tossing unexpected challenges or enticing diversions your way, yet ensuring allegiance to your financial blueprint means that the momentum of your financial snowball remains unimpeded.

One of the most profound enchantments of compound interest is its indifference to market oscillations or economic slumps; it perseveres, reliant solely on the passing of time, performing its task diligently in the backdrop. Incremental deposits, coupled with time, culminate in a financial metamorphosis—a garden you carefully nurtured evolving into a breathtaking floral masterpiece. So, embark on your savings journey promptly, adhere to it with unwavering consistency, and let compound interest manifest as your steadfast financial superhero. This unrelenting force quietly works in the recesses, ensuring your future is awash with possibilities and freedoms, crafting a reality where financial aspirations are accessible and attainable.

$$ LEVEL UP MONEY MOVES $$

1. ☐ Start your emergency Fund

Set aside a small amount religiously each week or month, dedicated explicitly to building your emergency fund. Write down your goal amount; visualize it vividly, and track your steady progress in a personal journal or through a digital financial app. Celebrate when you attain significant milestones like $100 or $200, acknowledging the personal dedication it required! Reflect on how having this buffer, this resolute safety net, elevates your sense of security and preparedness for the unexpected intricacies of life.

In the end, having an emergency fund is like possessing a financial safety net interwoven with assurance and reliability. It's thoughtfully there to catch you when life decides to nudge or even drastically throw you off balance. It empowers you to gracefully handle unexpected expenses with both grace and confidence. So, embark on building yours today; in the future, you will undoubtedly be grateful for your foresight and ddication!

2. ☐ **Create a fund for a big purchase** (e.g., a bicycle, scooter, or a trip)

Imagine casually strolling past your favorite music store, your eyes catching that sleek guitar sitting prominently in the window, its lustrous, polished finish practically whispering your name. Wind chimes hanging by the store door jingle harmoniously, complementing the allure of the beckoning instrument. Or perhaps it's not a guitar at all but the latest must-have gadget, an embodiment of modern technology's promise to elevate your lifestyle to unparalleled coolness. But hold your horses! Before you even consider the quick draw of your wallet, there's a fundamental conversation to be had about the art and cunning magic of planning for substantial purchases. Think of it as the meticulous crafting of a majestic sandcastle by the shore; without the architectural solidity of a well-thought-out plan, the grand edifice is sure to crumble at the first threatening crash of a wave. Meticulous foresight in budgeting for major expenses becomes your shield against the lightning impulsiveness of buying what could leave your financial reserves gasping for air. Moreover, when you deliberately save up prior to making a hefty purchase, you're effectively swimming clear of the tumultuous waters of debt, successfully evading the dreaded sensation of a financial hangover.

Establishing savings targets for these lustrous big-ticket items parallels plotting your adventurous route on a treasure map. Start by meticulously calculating the total eventual outlay for your dream item and decide upon a practical timeline to achieve your goal. Let's say that an enchanting guitar is priced at $600, and you aim to possess it within an ambitious yet achievable timeframe of six months—that's a targeted saving of $100 each month. Break this down into doable, bite-sized monthly savings, akin to slicing an enormous pizza into gratifying, manageable wedges. This approach ensures that you're not overwhelmed by the daunting figure, allowing you to maintain your focus on the prize without losing your momentum or spirit. By dissecting the colossal mountain into a series of approachable small hills, you transform what seemed like an insurmountable challenge into a feasible journey.

Tracking your progress is where the motivational wind takes your sails, propelling your voyage, much like witnessing your character ascend levels in a captivating video game. Utilize savings goal calculators to precisely ascertain your current stance towards achieving your cherished aspiration. Visual progress trackers enhance this journey splendidly. Picture a thermometer icon gradually filling as your funds accumulate, steadily creeping toward the marked target, or observe graphs that show how each deposit incrementally hones in on that epic acquisition. These tools aren't merely visually appealing; they serve as a constant and electrifying reminder of how far you've traversed and how tantalizingly close you are to seizing your dream. It's akin to having your personalized cheerleader cheering fervently from the sidelines, albeit sans the pom-poms.

Keeping your motivation ignited while on a saving spree can occasionally mimic watching paint dry—slow, seemingly endless, and monotonous. However, fret not, for there are delightful strategies to maintain your spirits vibrant and your enthusiasm pulsating. Celebrating milestones along your path is crucial. Do not wait until you've saved the entire desired sum to indulge in celebratory cheer; commend smaller triumphs along the journey. Perhaps at the halfway milestone, indulge in a cup of freshly brewed coffee or enjoy a cinematic adventure with friends. Visualizing the perquisites of your impending purchase also aids in sustaining the fire within. Visualize yourself jamming soulfully on that glorious guitar or harnessing that cutting-edge gadget every time the temptation to deviate from your savings looms. It's all about maintaining steadfast focus on the tantalizing prize that awaits.

When you embark on this enriching savings expedition, remember, it's not merely about depriving yourself of enjoyment; it's about implementing astute choices today for astonishing rewards tomorrow. And although the anticipation may be challenging, the elation of finally securing that sought-after purchase with cash you've diligently saved is insurmountably fulfilling. It's the embodiment of financial liberation, neatly wrapped in a glossy, appealing bow, promising you not just ownership, but the triumph of discipline and foresight realized.

3. ☐ Take the "College Savings Knowledge" quiz

Grab a piece of paper or open your notes app and jot down three steps you can take right now to start saving for college. Whether it's researching 529 plans or setting small monthly savings goals, these steps will set you on the path to education success.

Think of college savings as a strategic game where your opponent is potential debt, and your victory is financial freedom.

Understanding your options means you're equipped with the right tools to tackle those costs head-on. Starting early gives you a head start that compounds over time, reducing future headaches and opening doors to possibilities without financial shackles holding you back. Whether through structured plans like 529s or simpler methods like savings accounts, every dollar saved is one less dollar borrowed, allowing you to focus on hitting the books instead of worrying about bills.

Estimating expenses isn't just number-crunching; it's about anticipating needs and crafting a plan that aligns with your goals and resources. Scholarships and financial aid are not just mythical creatures; they're very real and within reach if you know where to look and prepare accordingly. So take these insights, arm yourself with knowledge and resources, and get ready to conquer the world of higher education without letting finances hold you back from achieving greatness!

4. ☐ Take on one of the Savings challenges mentioned below

Let's turn the otherwise boring topic of savings into a vibrant and challenging new world. A fascinating realm where the otherwise tedious task of saving transforms into an exhilarating competition. It infuses motivation and makes the entire process joyful and captivating. Imagine it somewhat akin to engaging in a friendly contest with yourself, where you get to set your sights on specific goals, meticulously track every step of progress, and bask in the delightful celebrations of each small victory. The excitement that stems from cultivating a competitive edge can propel you forward, encouraging you to save consistently and diligently. It's reminiscent of striving for a personal best in a beloved sport or activity. The more invested you become, the more your savings account flourishes.

Let's thoroughly explore some popular savings challenges that promise to invigorate your financial standing and give your piggy bank a robust and rewarding workout.

1. Kicking it off is the widely acclaimed **52-week savings challenge**. This challenge is not only simple but highly effective: commence by saving a modest $1 in the first week, gradually increasing to $2 in the subsequent week, and continue this increment each week. By the close of the year, your efforts will culminate in amassing a substantial sum exceeding $1,300.

2. Next, consider the **spare change challenge**—an ingenious approach that encourages squirreling away every coin each time you break a bill. You'll be amazed at the remarkable pace at which those seemingly inconsequential nickels and dimes multiply into a significant amount.

3. Now, for those seeking a more formidable test of resolve and determination, look no further than the **no-spend month challenge**. Select a particular month during which you commit wholeheartedly to spending solely on essentials. This is akin to embarking on a financial detox, cleansing and rejuvenating both your wallet and mind.

Embracing these challenges extends beyond merely enhancing your cash flow; it fosters invaluable traits such as discipline and deepens your financial awareness. These experiences teach you the importance of pausing thoughtfully before making impulsive purchases. You'll begin to ponder whether indulging in that extra-large latte is truly necessary or if your current phone case serves its purpose just fine. The more you push your limits and challenge yourself, the quicker you'll attain your savings aspirations. It's akin to unearthing a hidden gem, realizing that your potential to save surpasses your wildest dreams.

Crafting personalized savings challenges introduces an additional layer of enjoyment and inspiration. Tailoring these challenges to suit your lifestyle and unique financial circumstances can be incredibly motivating. For instance, you could resolve to save $5 each time you decide to refrain from a night out on the town, or perhaps set aside $10 every time you receive an A on a report card or achieve a fitness milestone. Unleash your creativity and watch it flourish! Involving friends or family members can significantly amplify the enjoyment and accountability of these challenges. Imagine instigating a savings challenge with your sibling to see who can accrue more savings by month-end; the one who saves less can humorously take on the other's household chores—that's some powerful motivation right there!

Personalized Challenge Ideas

Design a savings challenge that is uniquely yours by establishing rules that align with your spending and daily habits. Perhaps you wish to save each time you successfully resist the urge to purchase new clothes or decide to squirrel away cash whenever you hit your fitness targets. Make sure to document your rules and track your progress using an app or journal to ensure you remain committed and motivated.

Throughout this chapter, we've journeyed through an array of methodologies aiming at saving for both immediate objectives and long-term goals, underscoring the notion that even seemingly minor actions today can precipitate remarkable results in the future. As this segment draws to a close, bear in mind that these savings strategies transcend mere monetary accumulation; they're instrumental in fostering habits that pave the path to financial liberation. In the upcoming chapter, we will delve into insightful budgeting techniques designed to keep you aligned with your goals, ensuring your savings continue to grow steadily while you savor life's delightful luxuries along the way.

6

NAVIGATING CREDIT AND DEBT

CREDIT SCORES: THE BASICS AND WHY THEY MATTER

The credit world can seem confusing, but one of the most important things to understand is your **credit score**. It acts like a **financial report card**, showing how responsible you've been with money, things like paying bills on time or managing debt. Lenders, landlords, and even some jobs may look at your credit score to decide if they can trust you financially. The higher your score, the more opportunities you'll have. This number acts as a beacon for lenders, showcasing how likely you are to fulfill your financial obligations and repay what you owe them. Your credit score is calculated using two predominant systems, FICO and Vantage Score. Your credit score appears as a three-digit number ranging between 300 and 850, with higher scores being more desirable.

Credit Score	Rating	What It Means
800 – 850	Excellent	You're a financial rock star! You'll get the best interest rates and loan offers.
740 – 799	Very Good	Lenders see you as low risk. You'll likely get great loan terms
670 – 739	Good	You're doing well, but there's room to improve for better deals.
580 – 669	Fair	Some lenders might approve your application, but you may pay higher interest rates.
300 – 579	Poor	You'll likely be denied

Table 2: Credit Score Definition Table

But what exactly contributes to this enigmatic and magical credit score? **Payment history** is monumental—akin to a diligent student not being late to class, it serves as a testament to your reliability and trustworthiness. **Credit utilization** is another significant factor; it reflects the ratio between the credit you're using and the credit available to you. Imagine possessing a pizza and consuming half—that's 50% utilization, a concept that defines your financial prudence. Additional factors influencing your score include the **length of your credit history**, the **diversity in types of credit you utilize**, and **recent credit inquiries**. By keeping these elements aligned and in check, you actively maintain a healthy credit score that stands in your favor.

Possessing a stellar credit score is like wielding the golden ticket to the financial world. Such a score can significantly enhance your ability to **qualify for loans with lower interest rates**, thereby saving you enormous amounts over time in the form of interest payments that accrue. When the time eventually arrives for you to rent your first apartment or seize that dream job, a good credit score acts like a key that swings open those elusive doors. Interestingly, **many landlords and employers check credit scores** to gauge an applicant's trustworthiness, almost like sporting a badge that declares, "I'm responsible, hire me!"

If you're curious about obtaining your own credit score, the process is simple and very accessible. As a consumer, you're entitled to receive a free annual credit report from each of the three major credit bureaus —**Equifax, Experian**, and **TransUnion**. Simply visit **AnnualCreditReport.com** to access yours. For continual monitoring, consider utilizing services that track your score and send alerts regarding any changes. These can prove particularly beneficial if you're in the midst of improving your score or wish to preemptively catch and address identity theft.

Your credit score steers financial decisions more extensively than you might initially surmise. Banking institutions utilize it to make determinations regarding loan approvals and to set applicable interest rates. A high score can signify a higher credit limit—which can feel like receiving extra lives in a game—but always remember not to spend recklessly in the heat of the moment. Insurance companies, too, glance at your score to establish policy premiums, where maintaining a high score can translate to monetary savings there as well.

VISUAL ELEMENT: CREDIT SCORE FACTORS CHART

Consider creating a dynamic chart that vividly illustrates and delineates the factors that impact your credit score: payment history (35%), credit utilization (30%), length of credit history (15%), types of credit (10%), and new credit activity (10%). This visual tool serves to clarify and distill what carries the most significance in maintaining a healthy score, offering a user-friendly guide for better understanding.

Factor	What It Means	Impact on Score
Payment History	Do you pay your bills on time?	35%
Amounts Owed	How much of your credit limit are you using (also called credit utilization)?	30%
Length of Credit History	How long have you had credit accounts open?	15%
New Credit	How often do you apply for new credit (too many = risky)?	10%
Credit Mix	The variety of credit types you have (like credit cards, student loans, etc.).	10%

Table 3: Credit Score Factor Table

Your credit score is far more than just a numerical value; it's a profound and powerful tool in your financial toolbox. Grasping what affects it and comprehending why it holds significance places you at the helm of your financial journey. By **checking your score regularly**, remaining informed about how it impacts potential opportunities, and understanding the doors it might open, you're actively setting yourself up for success. So confidently embrace your inner financial explorer and let your credit score enthusiastically lead the way, ensuring you're prepared for the financial adventures that await!

GETTING YOUR FIRST CREDIT CARD: A BEGINNER'S GUIDE

You've just turned 18, and now you're stepping into adulthood—a stage of life filled with new responsibilities, opportunities, and decisions that can shape your future. A significant early decision you might face is acquiring your first credit card. You've probably seen credit cards in tons of movies and shows—used to buy everything from coffee to cars. But what do they actually do in real life, and why do they matter? **Credit cards let you borrow money to make purchases now and pay it back later.** Each time you use one, you're taking out a small loan from the bank or credit card company. If you pay the full amount back by the due date, you usually don't pay extra. But if you don't, they **charge you interest**—and that can add up fast.

Step 1: Should I get a Credit Card?

It depends on your money habits and how ready you are to take on the responsibility. A credit card can be a great tool for building your credit history, which is important for things like renting an apartment, getting a car loan, or even applying for certain jobs. **But it's not free money.** You have to pay back everything you spend, plus interest if you don't pay the full balance each month.

If you're someone who can stick to a budget, pay bills on time, and avoid impulse spending, then starting with a low-limit or student credit card could be a smart move. But if you're still learning how to manage money, it might be better to wait and start with a debit card to build good habits first.

Bottom line: Only get a credit card when you're confident you can use it wisely and not rack up debt.

Step 2: Practice fiscal responsibility with a Debit Card first

Before jumping into credit cards, it's smart to start with the basics, like using a **debit card** and creating a simple **budget**. A debit card pulls money directly from your bank account, so you're only spending what you actually have. It's a great way to learn how to track your spending, avoid overdrafts, and make thoughtful choices with your money.

Practicing fiscal responsibility means knowing where your money is going and making sure you're not spending more than you earn. Try making a basic budget by listing your income (like allowance, job pay, or gift money) and your regular expenses (like food, gas, subscriptions, or savings goals). Stick to it. Learning to manage money with a debit card and a budget builds the habits you'll need to handle bigger financial tools—like credit cards—later on, without falling into debt.

Step 3: When you are ready, Obtaining a Credit Card

Ok, now that you have practiced fiscal responsibility and are now ready to obtain and handle a credit card, what's next? How do I apply for a credit card?

1. **What type of credit card should I get?**

You want a card that harmonizes seamlessly with your lifestyle and aids your financial growth journey. Seek out options that offer low interest rates and do not have annual fees. Student credit cards are particularly advantageous if you're currently submerged in the academic world, providing perks designed with student life in mind. Lastly, if traditional credit cards seem just out of reach owing to eligibility constraints, consider secured credit cards as a viable stepping stone. These cards necessitate a deposit, which then serves as your credit limit, facilitating credit building without succumbing to the temptation of overspending. Engaging with reliable resources such as **Experian** can prove invaluable for acquiring insights into fostering a sound credit foundation.

2. **How to Apply for a Credit Card**

Navigating the credit card application process is not equivalent to cracking complex calculus, yet it does demand certain preparations.

   a. Begin by completing an application form, typically requesting essential information such as your name, address, income, and current employment status.
   b. In some instances, additional documentation may be required, such as proof of income or identification to ascertain your reliability. It can be likened to applying for a part-time job—you're fundamentally attempting to convey to the bank that you embody responsibility and trustworthiness. Post-submission, you embark on the

waiting game, akin to the anticipation surrounding exam results, yet tinged with more pronounced financial implications.

    c. You might get and instant answer, in some cases, you will have to wait for the response via email or regular mail.

    d. If approved, a credit card with your name on it will be shipped via US Mail.

3. **Using your Credit card**

    a. Once you receive your shiny new card in the mail, you must first activate it. There is usually a QR Code to activate it online. Instructions will be given on the white sticker on the card.

    b. Once activated, remove the white sticker and sign the back of your card

    c. Your card is now ready for use.

    d. When using it, you can either "tap" it on payment readers or slide the chip side first into a card machine.

    e. The merchant might possibly ask you to sign a copy of their receipt.

Now, it falls upon you to wield this newfound financial power with responsibility and foresight. **Paying off the full balance** of your card each month holds critical importance. Much like consuming your greens or hraving that early morning jog, it might not always come naturally or seem enjoyable, but it maintains financial well-being in the grand scheme. Abstain from opting for cash advances, which are essentially like pulling cash from your future self, complete with high accompanying fees. The allure may be strong, but these advances can easily lead to financial mire if approached carelessly. Maintain vigilant oversight over your statements to ferret out unauthorized charges. Opportunistic fraudsters lurk about, and identifying suspicious activity early can save you from potentially sticky predicaments.

Scenario: You walk into a store with the intention of purchasing a simple pack of gum. However, mere minutes later, you are at the checkout counter, arms full and your wallet significantly lighter, having collected a cart brimming with items like that novelty mug and the trendy hoodie. This is the sneaky art of overspending in action, my friend—a scenario all too familiar to many. It's one of the most common culprits leading individuals down the precarious path of debt accumulation. Pair this with those irresistible impulse purchases—the kind made in spur-of-the-moment excitement and enthusiasm, which seemingly seemed like a splendid idea until reality kicks in—and suddenly, you're staring at an alarming amount of spending. But wait, this journey doesn't end here! Another pathway down this road leads through reliance on credit for purchases that are far from essential. You use your credit cards as if they offer an unlimited reservoir of funds, without comprehending that the money you are spending is essentially a loan from your future self. Sadly, this future self will have to not only pay back this original purchase, but if you do not have enough in your bank account, when the monthly credit card comes due, you will be charged an exorbitant amount of interest on the balance, which you cannot pay.

Example: Donna's Credit Card Lesson

Donna got her first credit card in March with a **$1,000 limit**. She used it for everything—car repairs, gas, fancy coffee, lunch with friends, new clothes, and a couple of last-minute road trips. By the end of the month, she spent **$1,050**, which is **over her limit**.

Her bill came in, and it said she owed **$150 as a minimum**

payment, but she only had **$500** to put toward the total. That left **$550 unpaid**.

Because she didn't pay it all off, the credit card company charged her **27.9% interest** on the leftover $550. That's about **$153** in interest added to her balance.

So now, instead of just owing $550, she owes **$703**. And that's before she even starts using the card again the next month.

Bottom line: If you don't pay your full balance, interest adds up fast, and you end up paying way more than you spent.

The Cost of Not Paying It Off: Interest and the Debt Spiral

So, how does one navigate away from this looming trap and instead nurture flourishing finances? Let's engage in a dialogue on strategies for developing habits around healthier spending.

1. Use your debit card or cash whenever possible
2. If you choose to use your credit card (so that you can build up your credit score), begin by **setting firm spending limits** as if they are guardrails on a winding mountain road. These financial boundaries serve to keep you from veering off course into treacherous financial territories filled with uncertainty and stress. Most credit cards have the option of setting up spending limits. If you are nearing these limits, you can receive a warning text..
3. **Craft a budget** with precision and care, especially directed toward credit card expenses, assuring you are well aware of your monthly financial landscape. This strategic planning enables you to sidestep unpleasant surprises when the credit card bills strand you in disbelief. Make distinguishing between needs and wants a staple of your spending philosophy. Easier said than done when those dazzling sneakers—noteworthy for their style and panache—whisper your name as you pass by. Yet, carefully weighing what you

truly need against what merely seems pleasing can pivot your financial health toward a positive trajectory.

4. When using your credit card, only use it for items within your monthly budget (e.g., Gas) and track spending weekly.

Pro Tip: Already picked a budget tracking app in an earlier chapter? Go ahead and link your new credit card to it, just like you did with your bank account. This helps you see *all* your spending in one place, whether it's from your debit or credit card. Don't forget to check the app each week to stay on top of where your money's going.

Excessive debt can sneak up on you if you're not paying attention. It can seriously hurt your financial health, just like a cold that won't go away. One major consequence is damage to your **credit score**, which makes it harder and more expensive to borrow money in the future. A low credit score can limit your options, like getting approved for a car loan, renting an apartment, or even qualifying for a good interest rate. In short, the more debt you carry without a plan to pay it off, the tighter your financial situation becomes.

Instead of leaning heavily on credit to finance every purchase, consider embracing alternatives that won't mire you in debt's quicksand. Debit cards present a straightforward method of completing transactions using funds you already possess, offering a transparent view of your spending tendencies without accumulating unnecessary debt. Then there's the timeless charm of cash—its tangible and finite nature makes overspending more challenging when you literally witness your funds deplete with each transaction. And let's not forget the strategic move of saving prior to making significant purchases. Though it might demand patience, the satisfaction of buying something outright equates to conquering a critical boss level in a challenging game, eradicating the stress of contending with interest.

CREDIT MYTHS BUSTED: SEPARATING FACT FROM FICTION

When it comes to credit, there's a lot of misinformation out there. It's easy to get confused by common myths, just like the old rumor that swallowed gum stays in your stomach for seven years (which, by the way, isn't true). The credit world is full of similar myths that many people still believe. Let's clear up the confusion and break down what's fact and what's fiction.

Myth: An all-too-common myth is the belief that *checking your own credit score will result in a decrease of that score.* It's just like thinking that merely glancing at your report card will somehow manipulate your grades. In truth, when you check your own credit, it constitutes a soft inquiry, and it doesn't impact your credit score in the slightest. On the other hand, hard inquiries, which occur when you apply for loans or credit cards, can momentarily affect your score to a minor degree.

Myth: Moreover, there's the persistent myth that *closing old credit accounts will bolster your credit score.* At first glance, this might seem logical; the idea that possessing fewer accounts might equate to a healthier credit standing. However, in actuality, closing old accounts can indeed harm your score. This is primarily because it truncates your credit history. Your credit history functions much like a timeline that showcases your financial prudence; the longer and the more unblemished it is, the more advantageous it becomes. Consequently, it is beneficial to maintain those old accounts, especially if they're in good standing.

Navigating through the labyrinthine world of credit information can be particularly daunting, especially given the cacophony of myths circulating. How can you tell what's true and what's just noise? Start by consulting reputable financial websites—these can serve as your trusted sherpa through the tangled thicket of credit myths. Websites sponsored by governmental agencies or established financial institutions are typically some of the most reliable sources available. If you still find yourself beset with uncertainty, seeking advice from financial professionals who can provide tailored guidance is always a wise move. Think of them as possessing a meticulously drawn map when you find yourself lost in an uncharted wilderness.

Trusted Government Financial Agencies

1. **Consumer Financial Protection Bureau (CFPB)**
   - Helps protect consumers from unfair financial practices and offers tools to manage money wisely.
   - cfpb.gov
2. **Federal Trade Commission (FTC)**
   - Offers guidance on avoiding scams, understanding credit, and protecting personal information.
   - ftc.gov
3. **Federal Reserve (The Fed)**
   - Explains how the economy works, interest rates, and offers tools for learning about credit and saving.
   - federalreserve.gov
4. **Securities and Exchange Commission (SEC)**
   - Regulates investing and protects investors; great for learning about stocks, bonds, and markets.
   - investor.gov
5. **USA.gov – Money and Taxes**
   - A central hub for learning about taxes, credit, loans, and other money-related topics.
   - usa.gov/money
6. **MyMoney.gov**
   - A site created by the U.S
   - mymoney.gov

Reputable Financial Institutions

1. National Banks

These offer wide accessibility, online banking, and strong security:

- **Chase (JPMorgan Chase)**
- **Bank of America**
- **Wells Fargo**
- **Citi (Citibank)**
- **U.S. Bank**

2. Online-Only Banks

Known for low fees, high savings interest rates, and easy app access:

- **Ally Bank**
- **Capital One 360**
- **SoFi**
- **Discover Bank**
- **Chime** *(note: technically a fintech company partnered with banks)*

3. Credit Unions

Member-owned, often with more personal service and lower fees:

- **Navy Federal Credit Union**
- **Alliant Credit Union**
- **SchoolsFirst Federal Credit Union**
- **PenFed Credit Union**

4. Financial Institutions with Strong Educational Tools

These banks also provide solid financial literacy resources:

- **Capital One**
- **Bank of America**
- **Discover**

A meticulous understanding of credit is pivotal for making intelligent, well-informed decisions that can shape one's financial future. It's not solely about avoiding myths; it's also about grasping the realities of credit management. Credit-related laws and policies are subject to change, and staying abreast of these changes guarantees that you're perpetually one step ahead. Knowledge is indeed a powerful tool, especially when it comes to deciphering your credit reports and understanding their implications for your financial health.

As you navigate this complex journey of disentangling myths from facts, keep in mind that being well-informed stands as your most powerful weapon. So, the next time you encounter a credit myth, take a moment to pause and subject it to scrutiny. Immerse yourself in credible sources and gear up with the truth. Your financial future will express gratitude, allowing you to navigate the world of credit with newfound confidence and clarity, undeterred by the misleading shadows of misinformation.

Tackling this challenge requires proactive measures in the pursuit of accurate information and a critical evaluation of sources. It is vital not to accept anything at face value; delve deeper to unearth the truths that lie just beneath the surface. With each myth you debunk, you not only become wiser but also forge a path towards financial independence with every fact unearthed and comprehended.

So there you have it—credit myths busted wide open like a piñata at a lively celebration! Continue to question, continue to learn, and strive for that esteemed status of financial savvy. And who knows? You might discover that you've become the unofficial credit advisor in your network, the go-to person among your friends for all things credit-related!

DEBT IS *the biggest thief* OF YOUR FINANCIAL FUTURE.

— DAVE RAMSEY, PERSONAL FINANCE EXPERT

You might already have some experience with credit cards—and maybe even some debt—before picking up this book. If you're trying to work your way out of it, you're not alone. There are two popular ways to tackle debt: the **snowball method** and the **avalanche method**.

With the **snowball method**, you focus on paying off your **smallest debts first**. Each time you knock one out, you build motivation and confidence to take on the next. It's like winning small battles that give you the energy to face the bigger ones. This method helps you build momentum, which can make sticking to your plan a lot easier.

Now, meet the **avalanche method**. This one's for the thrill-seekers who want to face the steepest challenges head-on. Here, you focus on **debts with the highest interest rates first**. It's like going straight for the boss battle because you know that beating it will save you the most in interest payments, freeing up resources to tackle the rest. Both methods have their charm, so choose your adventure wisely.

Creating a debt repayment plan starts with getting organized. Begin by listing all your debts, including the interest rates and how much you owe on each. This gives you a clear picture of what you're dealing with and helps you decide where to focus first. Then, set aside a specific portion of your budget for paying down debt—treat it like an essential expense, like rent or groceries. Track your progress regularly and make adjustments if needed. Each payment you make brings you closer to being debt-free.

Consistency in debt repayment is key to conquering this mountain. Making regular payments helps reduce what you owe over time and keeps your progress steady. Set up automatic payments to avoid missing due dates and getting hit with late fees. If automatic payments aren't an option, set reminders on your phone or calendar so you never forget. Staying on top of your payments can save you money, reduce stress, and keep your financial goals on track.

Sometimes, even heroes need a little help from wise mentors. Enter **financial counseling services**—your Gandalf in this quest. These professionals can offer guidance tailored to your needs, helping you navigate rough patches with expertise and insight. Services like credit counseling provide personalized advice, assisting you in refining your repayment strategy and staying on course. Debt management programs offer structured plans that work with creditors to make your repayment journey smoother. It's like having a co-pilot who knows all the shortcuts and detours.

RESPONSIBLE BORROWING: MAKING SMART CHOICES

Let's talk about responsible borrowing—a skill that's all about taking out only what you know you can pay back without stress. It's important to understand that loans can be helpful tools, but only if you use them wisely. Before you agree to borrow money, make sure you fully understand the terms. That means knowing the interest rate, how much your monthly payments will be, and how long you'll be paying it back. Always read the fine print—hidden fees or conditions can show up there and cost you more later if you're not careful. Being informed is the best way to stay in control of your finances.

When it comes to evaluating loan offers, think of yourself as a meticulous detective on a critical mission. Your goal is to scrutinize every detail for clues hidden within interest rates and fees. Is one loan offer too good to be true? That could very well be the case! Compare several options to find the loan that suits your financial scenario best. Some offers may have enticingly low introductory rates with beautifully crafted advertisements, only to disguise skyrocketing fees or rigid guidelines. And about that all-important fine print—yes, it's often tedious, crammed with jargon that seems unintelligible at first glance, but it holds vital insights. Hidden fees can catch you off guard if you're not paying attention. Taking the time to understand what you're signing up for can help you avoid unexpected charges and keep your finances on track.

Borrowing isn't simply a means to obtain what you want now; it's a valuable pathway towards broader financial independence later. Responsible borrowing can be a key to unlocking doors to opportunities that once seemed tightly locked. A robust, positive credit history not only makes you appear trustworthy to future lenders but can also be enticing to potential landlords or business partners. It's like having a prestigious VIP pass granting you access to financial opportunities such as investments or perhaps even launching your own enterprise someday.

Now, consider how borrowing carefully impacts your future financial goals. It's all about balance, much like a daring tightrope walker holding a long pole, carefully inching forward with precision and grace. Borrowing for current needs should be a thoughtful process, ensuring it doesn't derail you from achieving future aspirations. Think twice before borrowing for non-essential items—those tempting impulse buys that seem absolutely crucial in the moment but often fade into obscurity over time. Keep in mind, every dollar borrowed must eventually be returned, frequently with a bit more tagged on due to interest as a reminder of the cost of borrowing.

Responsible borrowing transcends mere debt avoidance; it encompasses making astute choices today that will benefit and bolster your financial health tomorrow. It's akin to planting seeds for a flourishing garden you'll one day relish. Each decision casts an influence on your financial landscape, actively sculpting the opportunities and thwarting potential challenges that lie ahead.

So here we are at the grand culmination of Chapter 6, armed with the vital knowledge needed to navigate the formidable realms of credit and debt like a seasoned pro. Understanding responsible borrowing is comparable to possessing a trusty compass pointing you toward financial success. As we proceed on this enlightening journey, we'll explore ways to protect what we've diligently built and ensure the path of our financial journey remains as smooth and secure as possible. Get ready for Chapter 7 & Chapter 8, where we dive into the essentials of taxes and insurance—topics that might not sound thrilling at first, but are pivotal in keeping our financial house structurally sound and firmly in order!

$$ LEVEL UP MONEY MOVES $$

1. ☐ Complete the Credit Card Simulation Exercise

Let's introduce an engaging activity. Craft a mock budget encompassing hypothetical expenses—perhaps $100 for essential textbooks or $50 for those delectable late-night snacks—then track these expenditures utilizing a fictional credit card statement. As you observe how expenses accumulate over a given month, practice clearing the balance with "mock money." This exercise provides a tangible illustration of how swiftly minor purchases can add up and underscores the criticality of punctual bill payment.

Expense 1	_____	$_____
Expense 2	_____	$_____
Expense 3	_____	$_____
Expense 4	_____	$_____
	MONTHLY TOTAL	$_____

When wielded wisely, a credit card can unlock a world of opportunities rather than confining them behind closed doors. Mastery of this financial tool is about fostering balance—using it judiciously as an enabler rather than viewing it as an unending cash dispenser. As you venture through this intriguing dimension of adulthood, bear in mind that errors will occasionally occur, but seizing the lessons they offer is paramount. Think of your credit card as a powerful financial tool—not a free pass to overspend. When used responsibly, it can support your financial goals by helping you build credit, manage emergencies, and earn rewards. But it's essential to use it with care: only charge what you can afford to pay off in full each month, avoid high-interest debt, and always make payments on time. Used judiciously, a credit card can be a trusted ally on your path to financial strength and independence.

2. ☐ <u>Perform a spending habit audit</u>

Spend a generous chunk of time reflecting on your spending habits by conducting a comprehensive audit. For the upcoming week, diligently record every purchase, not excluding those spontaneous late-afternoon snack runs.

Pro Tip: Use the app you downloaded in Chapter 3 to track your expenses.

At week's end, sift through your list meticulously and categorize each item as a "need" or a "want." This introspective exercise provides significant insight into your expenditure patterns, fine-tuning your awareness of where your money diverges and spotlighting potential areas of improvement. Plus, it's a revealing exercise, uncovering patterns you never knew lurked beneath the surface.

Navigating through the intricate maze of financial choices needn't resemble maneuvering through an unsolvable puzzle. By recognizing common causes of debt and embedding healthier spending habits into your routine, you can preserve fiscal stability while circumventing the pitfalls leading to overwhelming debt. Always remember, it's all about balance and making informed choices that align harmoniously with your financial goals and aspirations. Therefore, let's strive to keep those wallets content and those debts expertly at bay!

3. ☐ Debt repayment checklist (if applicable)

Let's add a handy tool to your arsenal: a debt repayment checklist. Start by listing each debt, its balance, and interest rate. Note down payment due dates and amounts beside each entry. As you make payments, check them off with satisfaction. This visual tracker keeps you motivated and aware of your progress, turning what seemed impossible into an achievable goal.

Paid Off	Debt	Starting Balance	Interest Rate	Due Date	Minimum Payment
✓	e.g. Car Loan	$10,500	8.5%	1st	$350

Pro Tip: Use a debt tracking/debt repayment website to meticulously track your debt reduction.

a. Debt Payoff Calculator - Stress Proof Your Money. https://stressproofyourmoney.com/tag/debt-payoff-calculator
b. The Ramsey Solutions Debt Snowball Calculator
c. Debt Snowball Calculator - Ramsey

Debt may feel overwhelming, but it doesn't have to be a lifelong burden. With thoughtful planning and a little determination, you can chip away at it bit by bit until it's nothing more than a memory. Whether you're building momentum with the snowball method or tackling high-interest beasts with the avalanche approach, remember that each payment is a victory. Make consistency your ally and seek guidance when needed—you can achieve financial freedom.

And like all good adventures, this one comes with its share of challenges and triumphs. Embrace the journey, learn from each step, and celebrate milestones along the way. Before you know it, you'll be standing at the summit of your financial mountain, gazing out at new horizons filled with possibility and promise.

7

DEMYSTIFYING TAXES

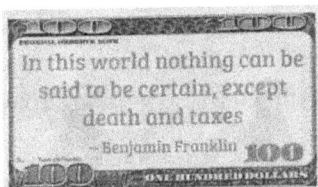

TAXES 101: WHAT TEENS NEED TO KNOW

Ever wonder who pays for your school, the roads you drive on, or the firefighters who respond to emergencies? It's not free, and that's where taxes come in. *Taxes are a portion of the money people earn, collected by the government to keep things running smoothly.* They help fund the services we all depend on every day. Without taxes, there'd be no one to fix potholes, teach in classrooms, or respond when you call 911. It's how we all chip in to keep our communities safe, functional, and fair.

"You can't avoid taxes, but you can get smart about them. The more you understand, the more control you have over your money."

— INSPIRED BY DAVE RAMSEY

So, what are these taxes we keep hearing about? Let's break them down.

1. **Income tax is the money you pay to the government based on how much you earn.** It's taken from your paycheck to help fund things like schools, roads, healthcare, and emergency services. The more you make, the more you're expected to contribute. It's not a punishment—it's how we all chip in to keep society running.
2. **Sales tax is added to the price of goods you buy**. That's why the $2 candy bar costs you a bit more at checkout.
3. And then there's **property tax, which is basically a fee homeowners pay to support local services** like fire departments and schools.

Now, let's dive into the nitty-gritty of **income tax**. Think of it as a tiered cake, where each layer represents a tax bracket. The more you earn, the higher up the cake you go. Tax rates increase with income, meaning those earning more pay a higher percentage. Don't worry; you don't jump into a higher bracket with every extra dollar you earn. Only the portion that exceeds each threshold gets taxed at the higher rate. Withholding is when your employer deducts tax from your paycheck to send directly to Uncle Sam. Then there are deductions—like coupons for taxes—that reduce your taxable income, potentially saving you some cash.

Understanding taxes is crucial for making informed financial decisions. Didn't know you could get penalized for underpaying taxes? Surprise! It's like returning a library book late and getting fined. But mastering taxes means avoiding these penalties and possibly getting a sweet refund come tax season. Knowing how taxes work helps you keep more of your hard-earned money and spend it on things you enjoy and want.

DECODING YOUR PAYCHECK: WHERE DID YOUR MONEY GO?

When you get your first paycheck, it might feel like a surprise—your take-home pay is less than expected. That's because certain taxes and deductions are automatically taken out before you even see the money. Understanding your paycheck and the taxes helps you know exactly where your money is going and exactly what to expect in your next paycheck.

Here's what to look for:

You'll usually see your **gross pay**, which is your total earnings before anything is taken out. Then come the deductions. **Federal income tax** is a big one—this goes to the U.S. government to pay for things like defense, healthcare, and national programs. You'll also see **Social Security tax**, which is part of **FICA** (Federal Insurance Contributions Act). This helps pay for retirement benefits and support for people with disabilities. Alongside that is the **Medicare tax**, also under FICA, which funds healthcare for seniors. These taxes are taken out of every paycheck—even if you're a teen—because they help support programs you might one day benefit from.

Here is an example of a paycheck stub (details about your earnings and deductions).

Sample Company Name
Sample Company Address
Sample Company Address Line2

Earning Statement
Check Number : #3456

Employee Details

Name	Employee Name	Employee ID	
Marital Status	Single	Exemptions	0
SSN	XXX-XX-	Reporting Period	01/01/1970 - 01/01/1970
Address	Employee Address Employee Address Line2	Pay Date	04/19/2018

Income		Year To Date		Deductions		YTD Total	
Rate	$10	YTD Gross	$6,400.00	Fica -Medicare	$5.80	Fica -Medicare	$92.80
Hours	40			Fica Social Security	$24.80	Fica Social Security	$396.80
Gross Earning	$400.00			Federal Tax	$35.82	Federal Tax	$573.12
				State Tax	$20.00	State Tax	$320.00

Current Pay	YTD Gross	Deductions	YTD Deductions
$400.00	$6,400.00	$86.42	$1,382.72

YTD Net Pay		Net Pay	
	$5,017.28		$313.58

Description	Amount	Deductions
Gross Pay	$1,000.00	
Federal Income Tax	($120.00)	Money taken from your paycheck by the U.S. government to help pay for national programs like defense, healthcare, education, and disaster relief. The amount you pay depends on how much you earn.
Social Security (FICA)	($62.00)	A government program that helps **support people who are retired, disabled, or have lost a working family member.** A small part of every paycheck goes into it to help others now—and you might benefit from it in the future.
Medicare (FICA)	($14.50)	A government health insurance program that helps cover **medical costs for people 65 and older**, and some younger people with disabilities. You help fund it through a small tax taken out of every paycheck—even as a teen worker.
State Income Tax	($30.00)	Money taken from your paycheck by your state government to help pay for things like public schools, roads, police, and local services. Not every state charges it, but if yours does, it helps keep your community running.
Other Deductions (e.g., 401k, insurance)	($50.00)	These deductions are optional and dependent upon your personal situation. For example, if you get employer sponsored health insurance, a portion might be deducted from your paycheck to pay for this.
Net Pay (Take-Home)	$723.50	This is the pay you will take home, after all deductions

Table 4: Paycheck deductions and taxes

FILING YOUR FIRST TAX RETURN: A SIMPLE GUIDE

Think taxes don't matter if you're not making much? Think again. You might've heard that you don't need to file a tax return if you don't earn enough—but here's the catch: even if it's not required, filing could actually put money back in your pocket. So before you skip it, let's break down why it might be worth your time.

For the tax year 2024, the **earnings threshold** for single individuals below 65 stands at an income exceeding $12,950. However, the intricacies of tax legislation don't halt at this singular point of reference. If you have a lucrative side hustle or partake in freelance work, those earnings also count toward your income. Even a seemingly negligible amount of $400, received from mowing lawns on weekends or selling your creative artwork online, is significant enough to demand reporting. Don't hesitate to reference the IRS website https://www.irs.gov/. There are interactive tax assistants, tools, and FAQs for just about every question you might have. There are also **free filing** options (for those making $84,000 or less).

Now, turning our attention to the detective tasks required to complete filing your tax return, first off, don't panic. There are many free resources to help you, as well as some super simple paid services. Check the "$$ Level Up Money Moves$$" at the end of this chapter for additional references to assist you.

Ready to take control of your taxes?

First, get your paperwork in order. Having the right documents on hand makes the process smoother and way less stressful. Here's what you might need (but the list can vary):

1. Income and tax Statements - Income, federal, and state tax details can be found on the **W2 Form.** This is a tax form your employer gives you (usually by the end of January) that shows how much money you made and how much taxes were taken out for the previous year. Your employer typically hands you a copy, mails it, or tells you how to access it via your online payroll portal (if your company has one).
2. Educational paperwork
   a. **Form 1098-T (Tuition Statement)** is a tax form sent to students by their college or university. It shows how much you (or your parents) paid for tuition and qualified education expenses during the year. This form helps you claim education-related tax benefits on your tax return. It can help lower the amount of taxes you owe—or even increase your refund.
   b. **1098-E (Student Loan Interest Statement)** is a tax form that your student loan provider sends to students. It shows how much interest you have paid on student loans. This form helps you claim education-related tax deductions.
3. Freelance or Gig Compensation—If you did freelance, gig work, or side jobs and earned $600 or more, you will receive a **1099-NEC** (Nonemployee Compensation) form.
4. Prize Money—The **1099-MISC** (Miscellaneous Income) reports other types of income, such as prize money, awards, or rental earnings.

5. <u>Savings & Investment Interest</u>—Your bank will send a **1099-INT** (Interest Income) if you earned interest from a savings account or other investments.

Time to Tackle Your Tax Form

Armed with these documents, it's now a matter of selecting the correct tax form for your needs. In most cases, the versatile **1040 form** will be the tool of choice for most taxpayers. If the sheer volume of paperwork seems overwhelming, envision it as selecting the most appropriate weapon in a dynamic video game, where each option serves a unique and strategic purpose.

The filing process doesn't culminate with merely selecting forms and gathering documents; you must proceed to the actual step of filing your tax return. Thankfully, various options are available to make this task seem less formidable. Online filing services such as **IRS Free File** offer free software, catering to those who meet specific income prerequisites. Consider this service as your personal assistant, effortlessly guiding you through each step of the filing process, with no extravagant fees becoming an unexpected burden! Alternatively, tax preparation software solutions like **TurboTax** or **H&R Block** come to the rescue, making the procedure seamless with their user-friendly interfaces. Think of them as a reliable GPS system, ensuring your tax journey remains free of wrong turns and missteps.

Lock It In: Submit Your Tax Return by April 15!

Accuracy in this domain becomes infinitely more crucial than perfecting the latest viral TikTok dance routine. The importance of filing your taxes with precision and in a timely manner cannot be overstated, as it plays an essential role in avoiding potentially unpleasant repercussions. The typical tax deadline occurs on April 15th—marking it on your calendar with the same enthusiasm and anticipation as a much-awaited concert date is crucial. Missing this designated deadline comes with the potential of facing penalties, such as fines or interest charges, a situation that can be likened to paying extra just for being late to the main event. Furthermore, errors within your tax return can invite audits or provoke delays in receiving refunds, reinforcing the need for utmost precision.

Conceive filing your taxes as akin to submitting a well-prepared homework assignment—execute it flawlessly, and you may find yourself rewarded with a refund; botch it, and you risk even more taxing work in the form of fines or amendments. Understanding these steps empowers you to navigate what might initially present as a daunting chore. Moreover, gaining mastery in this essential life skill early on establishes a solid foundation, positioning you favorably for financial success in the ensuing years! This journey through the labyrinth of tax filing, initially so seemingly overwhelming, becomes not only manageable but an empowering rite of passage into adulthood and fiscal responsibility.

$$ LEVEL UP MONEY MOVES $$

1. ☐ **Gather your Tax return paperwork (W2, 1099s, etc.)**
2. ☐ **File Federal Income taxes** – recommended free and paid resources below : **IRS:** https://www.irs.gov/how-to-file-your-taxes-step-by-step
   a. TurboTax: File Your Tax Return on the App Store
   b. **Taxact:** https://www.taxact.com/
   c. **FreeTaxUSA:** https://www.freetaxusa.com/
3. ☐ **File your state return** – Most filing software programs come with state filing programs as well. Don't forget this crucial step. You could be due even more of a refund from the state.

8

WHY INSURANCE IS RELEVANT FOR TEENS?

Insurance plays a crucial role in financial planning, acting as a buffer between you and unexpected expenses that could derail your financial goals. It ensures stability and protects assets during unforeseen circumstances. With insurance in place, you can focus on saving and investing without fear of losing everything due to an accident or illness. It's like having a sturdy umbrella during a rainstorm—you're prepared for whatever comes your way.

EVALUATING INSURANCE NEEDS: PROTECTING YOURSELF WISELY

Life can often feel like an intricate video game—just when you've acclimated to one level, a new challenge emerges, demanding fresh strategies and tools. In this metaphorical game, insurance stands as a critical asset, akin to armor that shields players from unforeseen threats. Constantly updating your insurance toolkit is essential as you progress through the various stages of life. Imagine landing your dream job, relocating to a bustling city, or finally purchasing that sleek vehicle you've been coveting. Each of these life milestones can influence your insurance requirements, much like equipping yourself with superior armor in anticipation of a formidable new boss. Keeping your coverage updated assures that you're well-protected against whatever adversities life may spring upon you. The essence lies in adapting seamlessly, ensuring that you're never caught unprepared by unexpected developments and can confidently manage the complexities life presents.

Embarking on an insurance needs assessment might initially appear as tedious as watching paint dry, perhaps even less thrilling than a repetitive task in a video game. However, its importance cannot be understated. Begin by meticulously reviewing what you've already acquired. Dust off those policy documents and scrutinize them to discern what's specifically covered and what's not, much like conducting an inventory audit before embarking on an adventurous quest. This foresight prevents scenarios where you suddenly realize the absence of a crucial item just when you need it the most. Identifying coverage gaps is vital; for instance, you don't want to find out that your renters' insurance fails to protect your precious collection of high-end electronics just when an incident occurs, or that your health plan inadvertently leads to significant out-of-pocket expenses. Early detection and rectification of these gaps safeguard you from potential issues becoming real-world headaches.

Now, parsing through an insurance policy's dense wording might make it seem as though it's composed in an arcane language, teeming with jargon and minuscule legalese. This is where the expertise of a seasoned professional becomes invaluable. Consulting an insurance agent is akin to seeking guidance from a sagacious mentor who adeptly navigates you through the labyrinth of policy intricacies. They possess the acumen to unravel the enigmatic fine print and furnish insights into coverage options that best align with your evolving needs. Moreover, they remain attuned to the latest developments and shifts in the insurance landscape—having such knowledge constitutes a formidable advantage on your side.

Yet, what if you find yourself inadequately covered? Welcome to the daunting territory of underinsurance—akin to braving a video game's hard mode without the requisite gear. Such a situation leaves you vulnerable and exposed, often finding yourself scrambling to address financial calamities that should have been cushioned by insurance. Conversely, there exists the peril of overinsurance. Imagine wearing so much protective gear that it impedes movement and slows your progress—this signifies unnecessary expenses sapping your resources and restraining your cash flow. Mastering the equilibrium of balanced coverage is imperative—you aim to be sufficiently protected without the burden of feeling encumbered by hefty premiums.

In summary, evaluating your insurance needs constitutes remaining agile and poised. Life unfailingly presents unexpected turns, but with comprehensive coverage in place, you're braced for any eventuality. Whether it entails adapting to life's transformations, soliciting expert counsel, or circumventing the hazards of under- or overinsurance, remaining proactive ensures you're in command. Insurance transcends being an obligatory expense; it emerges as your safety net, empowering you to navigate life's pursuits with unwavering assurance.

Now let's chat about the types of insurance that might actually matter for you. **Health insurance** tops the list. It's like a subscription to a healthcare safety club—you pay a monthly fee, and in return, you get coverage for doctor visits, medications, and more. Then there's **auto insurance**, especially if you're hitting the road. This one's a must-have, covering damages if you find yourself in a fender bender. And if you're living on your own or heading to college, **renters' insurance** is worth considering. It protects your stuff if something goes wrong, like a break-in or fire.

Choosing the right insurance is like picking out the perfect outfit—you want it to fit well and suit your needs. Start by evaluating what coverage you truly need. Are you accident-prone, or do you have health issues that require regular doctor visits? Compare policies by considering premiums—the amount you pay regularly—and deductibles—what you pay before insurance kicks in. It's like shopping around for the best deal without compromising on quality. Be sure to read the fine print, too. Policies can be tricky with their terms and conditions.

Insurance isn't just about paying premiums and hoping for the best. It's a key player in your financial strategy. Balancing coverage with budget constraints is crucial. You want enough protection without emptying your bank account. Think of it as finding the sweet spot between being covered and not overpaying for things you'll never use. Understanding policy terms helps avoid surprises later on. You don't want to find out an essential service isn't covered when you need it most.

Insurance might sound like a boring adult thing, but it's actually an empowering tool that gives you control over life's uncertainties. It's all about being prepared and making informed decisions to protect yourself and your future. By understanding the different types of insurance available, evaluating coverage needs, and incorporating insurance into your financial strategy, you can confidently navigate life's ups and downs without worrying about unexpected costs throwing you off course.

So next time someone mentions insurance, remember it's not just paperwork and premiums—it's your ticket to peace of mind while tackling the adventure we call life!

> *Pro Tip:* Use an online coverage checkup, such as Coverage Checkup - Ramsey, to learn your insurance needs. Many won't apply until later in your teens or even into your 20s.

HEALTH INSURANCE BASICS: NAVIGATING YOUR OPTIONS

Health Insurance is a critical component of the money game. Its purpose is to protect you from unexpected, high medical costs due to illness and injury. It can also give you access to preventive care, keeping you healthy without breaking the bank. Understanding health insurance terms is crucial so that you can learn how to select the right plan.

1. **Premiums** are what you pay monthly for coverage,
2. **Deductibles** are what you pay before insurance kicks in. For example, let's say you broke your leg and had to go to the emergency room to set it and cast it. Let's say the emergency room bill came to $2,000. Let's also say your health insurance deductible of the plan you selected was $250, you would be responsible for paying the hospital $250, while the health insurance company would pay the hospital the remaining balance of $1,750
3. **Copayments** are fixed amounts for certain services. For example, when visiting your doctor for a wellness check, a co-pay might be set at $50. No matter the cost of this visit (the insurance company will pay your doctor), you are responsible for paying your doctor $50. Typically, the medical facility

(doctor, lab, or hospital) requires this co-pay up front, at the time of the visit.

4. **In-network** providers are preferred doctors covered by your plan, while **out-of-network** ones might cost more. Please note that some health insurance plans might not cover any cost for out-of-network providers, so know your plan and coverage and beware of what you are responsible for.

There are several types of plans: **employer-sponsored ones through your job** or **parents'** work, **individual marketplace plans** for solo coverage seekers, and **Medicaid** or **CHIP** for eligible teens needing assistance. Choosing the right plan involves assessing healthcare needs and comparing benefits with costs. Use these resources to assist you in selecting the right plan for you.

Get Health Insurance Quotes From RamseyTrusted Experts - Ramsey

https://www.nerdwallet.com/article/health/choose-health-insurance?msockid=14fa12cb0e7360002974002d0f746198

AUTO INSURANCE: WHAT FIRST-TIME DRIVERS SHOULD KNOW

Auto insurance is a must-have if you own, lease, or even use your parents' car. It protects against damage and liabilities on the road. Mandatory **liability coverage** covers costs if you're at fault in an accident. **Premiums** depend on factors like your driving record and vehicle type—safe driving habits can lead to lower costs. Choosing auto insurance involves evaluating coverage options and significantly impacts your premium (the amount you pay each month). Typically, insurance companies have cost calculators that can show you the amount of coverage, deductibles, and premiums.

Each state has its own rules about how much coverage you need, so it's important to know what's required where you live. But auto insurance isn't just about covering damages from accidents. It also helps with theft and vehicle damage, offering peace of mind if your car decides to take a spontaneous vacation without you.

Now, let's talk about what affects those dreaded premiums—the amount you pay for this safety net. Your driving record is a biggie. If you've got a clean slate, insurers see you as less risky and might cut you some slack on costs. But if you've had a few too many speeding tickets or fender benders, expect your premiums to climb. Experience matters too; new drivers often face higher rates because, well, practice makes perfect, and lack of practice makes for higher insurance costs. The type of car you drive plays a role, too. Insurers consider how likely it is to be stolen or how much repairs might cost. Driving a flashy sports car might look cool, but it could burn a hole in your wallet when it comes to insurance.

- **Policy** - A legal contract between you and an insurance company. It outlines what is covered, what is not covered, how much the insurance company will pay, and how much you have to pay.
- **Premiums** – The amount you pay each month for the policy
- **Deductible** – The amount you must pay when invoking a claim (accident or damage). The insurance company pays the rest.
- **Bodily Injury Liability Coverage** – It pays for injuries you cause to others.
- **Property Damage Liability Coverage** – It pays for damage caused by someone else's car or property.
- **Collision Coverage** - It **pays to repair or replace your car** if it's damaged in a crash, regardless of who was at fault.
- **Comprehensive Coverage** - covers non-collision events. This coverage helps **pay to repair or replace your car** if it's damaged by something **other than a collision**.

Pro Tip: Reducing premiums can be achieved through good student discounts or safe driving programs. These programs are put in place to reward responsible driving

Evaluating insurance needs regularly ensures adequate protection as life changes occur, such as new jobs or moving to new cities. Conduct assessments by reviewing existing policies and identifying gaps where additional coverage might be necessary.

Pro Tip: Many reputable auto insurance companies offer free quotes, and some even send you comparisons against their competitors (such as Progressive). Get a quote from at least three companies before deciding.

So there you have it—the lowdown on auto insurance for first-time drivers. It's not just about ticking a box to get on the road legally; it's about safeguarding yourself from unexpected costs that could derail your finances. Understanding how premiums are calculated helps you make informed decisions when choosing coverage. And by exploring ways to reduce costs, you can keep more money in your pocket without skimping on protection. Auto insurance might seem like an annoying grown-up thing at first glance, but it's really about giving yourself the freedom to enjoy the ride without worrying about what-ifs lurking around every corner.

And hey, while we're on the topic of insurance, remember that being informed is your best tool for making smart decisions. Whether it's comparing coverage options or finding discounts that suit your lifestyle, taking charge of your auto insurance means you're not just along for the ride—you're in control of it!

As we conclude this chapter, it's beneficial to integrate these insights with your broader financial vision. Insurance is not an isolated tool; it's a salient component of a grander scheme to fortify a secure future. Once the appropriate coverage is established, you can channel your focus towards other financial ambitions—whether that involves bolstering savings, making prudent investments, or organizing an epic road trip with friends! In our next segment, we'll delve into strategizing for the future through savings and investments. Stay tuned, as the journey promises even greater insights ahead!

1. ☐ <u>**Perform an insurance coverage checkup assessment**</u>

Create an insurance needs checklist to evaluate personal coverage requirements based on current life circumstances. The checklist should include reviewing existing policies, identifying protection gaps, and consulting with a trusted insurance agent for guidance on complex details.

Understanding the balance between underinsurance—leaving yourself financially vulnerable—and overinsurance—unnecessary expenses—is crucial for comprehensive protection without breaking the bank.

2. ☐ **Purchase the insurance and add the cost to your monthly budget**

Use one of the handy online tools mentioned earlier in this chapter to find the best insurance companies and rates.

3. ☐ **Reconfigure budget savings and expenses to include this additional cost**

9

INTRODUCTION TO INVESTING

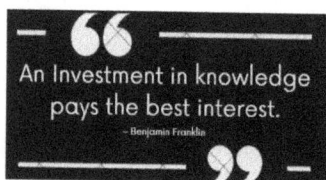

> An Investment in knowledge pays the best interest.
> – Benjamin Franklin

Investing is a powerful way to make your money grow over time. Instead of sitting in a savings account, your money is put to work to increase its value. This chapter is the tip of the iceberg when it comes to investing. Since this is a beginner's guide, do not expect too much detail. If you are interested in this topic and would like to explore it further, please check the end of this chapter for more in-depth resources.

Investing is about being intentional—choosing opportunities where your money can earn more, whether through stocks, bonds, real estate, or other assets. Unlike saving, which keeps your funds safe but relatively static, investing aims to build wealth and protect against risk by spreading your money across different types of investments. This strategy, known as **diversification**, helps reduce the impact of a loss if one investment doesn't perform well due to economic changes.

Starting early can make all the difference in the world. If you remember the concept of compound interest taught in the Savings chapter, it also applies to investing. The earlier you invest confidently, the more time you have to allow **compound returns** to work their remarkable magic. It is quite literally like a snowball energetically rolling down a hill, steadily gaining more snow, mass, and momentum as it rolls (Investopedia, n.d.). This compounding effect is one of the most remarkable ways to build financial independence and security over time. Think of it as planting a money tree. You nurture it thoughtfully, let it grow meticulously, and eventually, it bears fruit that can graciously support you in the future with a sturdy canopy of financial security.

Let's delve deeper into the nitty-gritty with some fundamental investment concepts. First up, we have **asset classes**. These are insightful categories of investments that include:

- **Stocks,** which are pieces of companies or ownership stakes;
- **bonds,** which are loans to companies or governments with the promise of future repayment;
- **real estate**, which typically refers to investing in properties.

Each carries its unique risk level and potential reward or return. Next, consider the **investment horizon**—this refers to the timeframe you plan to keep your money invested before you anticipate needing it. Whether you're aiming for short-term gains or long-term savings for retirement, your personal goals will shape your tailored investment strategy.

Okay, so you're ready to start investing—awesome! But where do you begin?

Step 1: First and most important, **research** your options diligently! Get familiar with various investment types and decide what resonates with your aspirations and risk tolerance. Do you want to invest in the world of company stocks or perhaps gravitate towards something steadier, with the predictability of bonds? Remember, ask trusted adults, financial advisors, and trusted online resources before investing any of your money.

Step 2: The next step is to realistically answer the question, **what amount of money am I willing to risk?** Because, although there are many investments out there that are extremely low risk, there is still always a risk of losing money.

Step 3: Once you've rolled up your sleeves and done your homework, the next essential step is **enrolling in a brokerage account.** This is where your investments live and thrive. Many platforms cater wisely to young investors, making it accessible and straightforward to get started with a bit of parental guidance. You'll need some basic info and possibly a parent or guardian's assistance if you're under the age of 18.

RISK AND REWARD: UNDERSTANDING INVESTMENT BASICS

Imagine strapping into a roller coaster: heart racing, palms sweating, anticipation building. Investing carries a similar thrill. Risk and reward are like two sides of a coin, intimately linked in a chaotic dance. The higher the risk, the greater the potential reward. Imagine betting on a new tech startup with a product that could change everything. If it succeeds, your investment might skyrocket, but if it flops, you could lose a chunk of your cash. It's all about balancing that adrenaline rush with your comfort zone.

Every investor faces different types of risks. Market risk is like the weather; it changes and can get stormy unexpectedly. One day, stocks are up; the next, they're down. Then there's inflation risk, which is sneaky. It's like the price of chips at your favorite store increases while your allowance stays the same, eroding purchasing power. Interest rate risk is another player in this game, impacting bond values when rates rise or fall. Each risk has its quirks, and understanding them helps you navigate the investing landscape like a seasoned explorer.

Finding your personal threshold for risk is crucial. You don't want to feel like you're riding a roller coaster if you're more of a merry-go-round type. Tools like **risk tolerance questionnaires** can help gauge your comfort level. These quizzes ask how you'd react to losing money or how much risk you're willing to take for higher returns. Keep in mind your time horizon, too—if you're saving for college, short-term fluctuations might not matter as much as long-term growth.

To balance risk and reward effectively, consider setting investment goals that align with your risk tolerance. Are you saving for something short-term, like a new laptop? Maybe go for safer investments. But if you're thinking long-term—say retirement—taking on more risk can lead to greater rewards over time. It's about finding that sweet spot where your goals and comfort level meet.

Remember that investing isn't about eliminating risk but managing it wisely. Like in life, where you take calculated risks every day—crossing the street, trying new foods—investing involves making informed choices. The more you understand risks and rewards, the better you'll be equipped to make smart investment decisions.

STOCK MARKET BASICS: THE TEEN'S GUIDE

Let's talk stock market. This isn't a mysterious Wall Street lair where only adults in suits can tread. It's a giant marketplace where people buy and sell shares of companies, like trading cards, but for grown-up companies. The stock market is like a bustling bazaar, buzzing with energy, where you're not just buying part of a company but a tiny slice of its future. These shares, or stocks, represent ownership in a company. If the company does well, your slice could become more valuable. These transactions happen on **stock exchanges**, places like the New York Stock Exchange (NYSE) or NASDAQ, which act like giant matchmakers pairing buyers with sellers.

Deciphering stock quotes and indices might seem like cracking a code, but it's simpler than you think. A stock quote gives you the latest price at which a stock is trading. Symbols like AAPL for Apple or MSFT for Microsoft are stock symbols that identify companies. Next, check out the price; this tells you how much you'd pay for one share. Market indices like the S&P 500 or NASDAQ are like report cards for the stock market. They track the performance of a group of stocks to give you a sense of how the market is doing overall.

Buying and selling stocks is like ordering your favorite pizza online —it's about making the right clicks. First, you need a broker. Think of them as your personal shopper in the stock market world. You tell them what you want to buy or sell, and they place the order for you. When it comes to placing orders, you'll encounter terms like "bid" and "ask" prices. The bid price is what buyers are willing to pay for a stock, while the ask price is what sellers want to get. Your broker helps you navigate this, ensuring you get the best deal possible.

So why invest in stocks? If you're looking for high returns, stocks have historically outperformed other investments over time. But remember, with high potential comes high risk. The stock market can be as unpredictable as your cat on catnip—one moment soaring, the next plummeting. Market volatility means prices can fluctuate wildly in short periods. It's like riding a roller coaster; thrilling but not for the faint-hearted. But here's the thing: investing in stocks isn't about making quick money. It's about playing the long game, riding out the ups and downs to achieve financial growth over time.

While the profit potential can be alluring, it's crucial to recognize that investing in stocks means accepting the inherent risks involved. One moment you're on top of the world with your stocks hitting new highs; the next, a market downturn leaves you wondering what happened. That's why having a diversified portfolio—spreading investments across various assets—can help cushion against the stock market's wild swings.

Understanding these basics is your entry ticket into the intriguing world of stocks. It's about making informed choices and not just following trends blindly. By grasping how stocks work and what influences their prices, you're better equipped to make decisions that align with your financial goals. Think of it as learning to ride a bike; wobbly at first, but smoother as you go along.

Investing in stocks isn't just for seasoned pros—it's an opportunity for anyone willing to learn and take calculated risks. With patience and continued learning, you can navigate this landscape confidently. Remember that every successful investor started somewhere, often with curiosity and a willingness to explore new horizons.

So, grab that metaphorical helmet and prepare for an adventure in the dynamic stock market world, where each trade is a step toward financial growth and understanding.

EXPLORING MUTUAL FUNDS AND ETFS

Next up are Mutual Funds and ETFs (Exchange-Traded Funds). These investment vehicles are tools that pool money from many investors to buy various assets, creating a diversified portfolio. You can reduce the risk significantly by having diversified investments within this one type of investment. Think of it as a basket filled with different fruits; if one goes bad, you still have plenty to enjoy. These funds are managed by financial professionals who choose and oversee the investments. Mutual funds are typically bought and sold at the end of the trading day and are designed for long-term growth. Conversely, ETFs can be traded throughout the day like individual stocks, offering more flexibility.

Mutual funds and ETFs offer a smorgasbord of benefits, especially for young investors venturing into the investment scene. For one, they provide diversification—spreading risk across various investments, which can lower the impact of any single underperforming stock. Plus, having professional managers means you don't have to sweat over daily market fluctuations. They do the heavy lifting so you can focus on other pursuits, like perfecting your TikTok dance moves or conquering that next level in your favorite game.

Choosing the right mutual fund or ETF requires some detective work. Consider the fund's performance history because you wouldn't want to ride a roller coaster that's been known to break down mid-loop. Check out the fees too; no one likes surprise charges sneaking up on them like a stealthy ninja. Align your choices with your investment goals and risk tolerance. If you're saving for something big in the future, like college or a dream trip, you might prefer funds that align with those timelines and risk levels.

Want to grow your money without stressing over stock picking?

Index funds are a smart, low-key way to invest. Instead of trying to beat the market, they match it, tracking big indexes like the S&P 500 or NASDAQ. That means you're investing in a bunch of top companies all at once, with low fees and less hassle. It's called passive investing, and it's all about steady growth without the drama.

The beauty of index funds lies in their simplicity and cost-efficiency. By tracking market indices, they offer broad diversification without requiring constant attention. It's like setting your phone to silent mode during class—you know it'll be there when you need it without causing unnecessary distractions. Index funds are often favored by those who prefer a hands-off approach or those just dipping their toes into the investing pool.

Investing in mutual funds, ETFs, or index funds doesn't require you to become a Wall Street guru overnight. It's about understanding these tools and how they can fit into your financial puzzle. Whether saving for college tuition or simply looking to grow your wealth over time, these investment vehicles offer accessible paths for achieving your goals. Explore options, ask questions, and remember that investing is not just about making money—it's about building a foundation for future adventures and dreams. But remember to check the costs of these, especially the fees.

Take a look at the simple chart below comparing average fees for mutual funds and ETFs. It highlights how even small differences can impact long-term returns. This visual can help you see why monitoring fees are crucial for maximizing your investment gains.

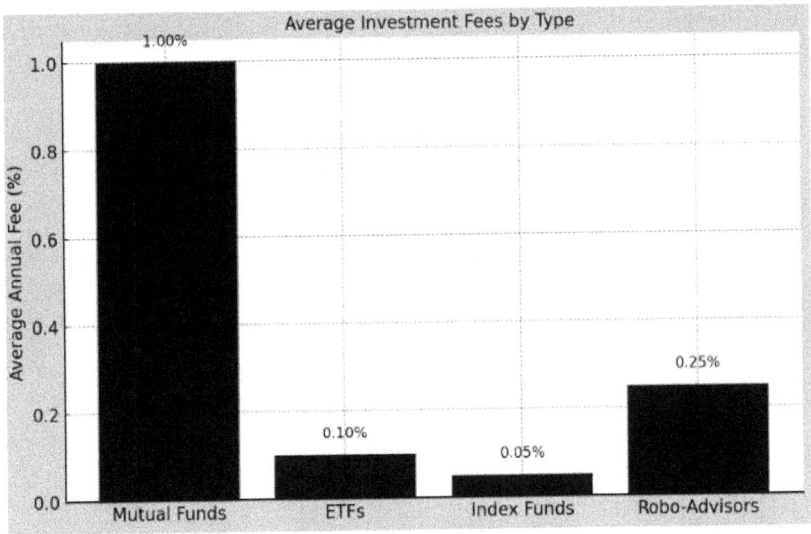

Average Investment Fees by Type

Graph 1: Investment fees by type

INVESTING IN YOURSELF: EDUCATION AND SKILLS

Setting educational and skill development goals might sound like homework, but think of it as plotting the ultimate quest. First, identify what you want to improve. Maybe it's that nagging feeling that you could be better at public speaking, or you want to learn graphic design. Once you've pinpointed your target, look for courses or workshops that align with your goals. Online platforms like Coursera or Skillshare offer a plethora of options, making it easier than ever to learn at your own pace. Set clear objectives and track your progress like you would in a game—each milestone is a victory worth celebrating.

In today's fast-paced world, lifelong learning is crucial. It's like keeping your operating system updated so you don't crash when new tech rolls out. Adapting to new technologies and industries is key to staying competitive in the job market. The skills you learn today might be outdated tomorrow, so keeping up is not just beneficial—it's necessary. Continuous learning helps you pivot when industries shift and ensures you're always on your game. Whether learning about AI or understanding the latest social media trends, staying informed keeps you relevant.

Success stories abound when it comes to self-investment. Take Sarah, who felt stuck in her admin job but had an eye for detail. She took a digital marketing course, which led to a new role in a trendy startup. Her salary doubled, and she now loves what she does. Or consider Mark, who always had a knack for storytelling but never pursued it seriously. After attending a few workshops, he became a freelance writer and now travels while working remotely. These aren't fairy tales; they're real outcomes of investing in personal growth.

INVEST IN YOURSELF TO GROW YOUR INCOME: A CASE STUDY

Investing in yourself through education and skills builds real power—it boosts your confidence, opens doors, and sets you up for bigger opportunities down the road. It's about boosting your stats to get that dream job or snag a promotion. When you learn new skills, you're not just adding bullet points to your resume but opening doors to endless opportunities. Whether it's coding, design, or mastering the art of negotiation, these skills can enhance your career prospects and, let's be real, fatten up that paycheck.

Meet Jenna, who adored photography but never saw it as more than a hobby. She started getting gigs after taking online courses and building an Instagram portfolio. Today, she's a sought-after photographer with clients worldwide. It's not just about luck; her dedication transformed passion into a thriving career.

The beauty of investing in yourself is that it's an **investment with guaranteed returns**. While stock markets fluctuate and economies sway, your acquired skills and knowledge stay with you forever. Education isn't just about degrees or certificates; it's about enhancing your ability to think critically and adapt swiftly. By focusing on personal development, you equip yourself with the tools to navigate life's challenges and seize opportunities that come your way.

Remember, every expert was once a beginner. The path may seem daunting initially, but with each step, you gain confidence and clarity in your abilities. The world is full of resources waiting for you to tap into them—books, podcasts, online tutorials, and mentors who can guide your journey. Approach learning with curiosity and enthusiasm, and you'll find that the possibilities are limitless. By investing in yourself today, you're creating a future where you're not just surviving but thriving in whatever field you choose.

Avoid thinking of personal development as a chore; see it as an adventure with endless potential outcomes. Whether mastering guitar chords or understanding quantum physics (okay, maybe not that extreme), every bit of knowledge adds to your arsenal. Keep exploring new horizons and embrace the changes that come with continuous learning. After all, the most exciting quests are those where we discover unknown parts of ourselves along the way.

ETHICAL INVESTING: MAKING A POSITIVE IMPACT

Investing is a way to grow your bank account and make the **world a better place**. That's what ethical or socially responsible investing is all about. Ethical investing is all about putting your money behind companies that care about the planet, their workers, and doing the right thing. Think clean energy, fair treatment, and real change. It's a way to support what matters to you while still growing your money.

Investing ethically doesn't just make you feel warm and fuzzy; it can spark significant change. When you invest in companies committed to doing good, you encourage corporate responsibility. Think of it as giving a nod of approval to businesses that consider their impact on society and the environment. Over time, this kind of investing can lead to long-term financial benefits for you and societal gains for everyone. Companies focused on sustainability often outperform in the market because they think ahead, innovate, and build loyal customer bases who appreciate their values. It's like getting a win-win of financial gains and contributing to a healthier planet.

So, how can you tell if an investment is actually ethical?

Start by looking into how a company operates, not just what they say in ads. Check if they're open about their practices and whether trusted sources support their claims. You can also explore ethical investment funds. These companies are chosen because they meet high standards for how they treat people, the planet, and how they're run. These funds help you invest in what matters to you, without doing all the research yourself.

Ethical investing is about creating synergy between personal beliefs and financial decisions. It's not just about making money; it's about making money matter. By supporting companies that prioritize ethics and sustainability, you're contributing to a future where businesses thrive without compromising the planet or people's well-being. As more investors demand accountability, companies are encouraged to adopt better practices, leading to broader societal shifts towards sustainability and responsibility.

So, why not let your investments echo your values? Ethical investing is an empowering way to take charge of your financial future while leaving a positive mark on the world. It's about using your resources to shape a future you're proud of—one where success is defined not just by profit margins but by the impact on communities and ecosystems.

As we wrap up this chapter, remember that ethical investing isn't just a trend but a movement towards conscious capitalism. By choosing where your money goes with intentionality, you're actively participating in shaping a world that reflects the values you care about most. Next, we'll explore how to keep your investments secure and make informed decisions that align with your long-term goals because being smart with money is just as crucial as being compassionate.

1. ☐ Assess your investment risk level

Take a moment to reflect on your own comfort with risk. Are you someone who loves adventure and is willing to take chances for big rewards? Or do you prefer a steadier path with fewer surprises? Jot down thoughts about what makes you nervous or excited about investing and consider how this might shape your investment strategy.

By exploring the world of investing with an open mind and understanding the dynamics of risk and reward, you're setting yourself up for financial success. It's like learning to ride a bike —you start wobbly but gain confidence as you go along. Embrace the journey, stay informed, and watch your investing skills grow alongside your confidence.

2. ☐ Scavenger Hunt Exercise to Find Investment Opportunities

Grab a notebook or digital tool, and jot down three companies or industries that intrigue and captivate you. Conduct thorough research on their stock performance over the past year and note any significant trends, shifts, or news that may have appreciably impacted their value. This exercise will help you practice analyzing potential investments critically and get more comfortable with how markets operate and fluctuate.

Remember, investing isn't a one-size-fits-all endeavor. It's personal, deeply personal, and should align with your unique financial goals and comfort level with risk-taking. Stay informed by regularly reading up on market trends and financial news—think of it as getting the inside scoop on what's hot or passably not in the dynamic, sometimes tumultuous investing world. By dedicating time and mustering patience, investments can undeniably become a powerful tool for building wealth and achieving financial freedom. So, keep your eyes on the prize, and happy investing, adventurer!

10

CYBERSECURITY: KEEPING YOUR FINANCES SAFE ONLINE

IS MY FINANCIAL AND PERSONAL INFORMATION SAFE?

Think your personal info is safe online? Think again.

Cybercriminals constantly find new ways to break into accounts and steal data, from stolen credit card numbers to full-on identity theft. This isn't just stuff you hear about—it's real and can happen to anyone. So, how do you protect yourself from being the next target? Let's break down these threats and the smart moves you can make right now to keep your info and money safe. Let's discuss some common cyber threats because awareness is your first line of defense.

1. **Phishing scams** are fake messages, usually emails, texts, or DMs, that trick you into clicking a link or giving out personal info like your passwords, bank details, or login info. They often look like they're from a real company (like your bank, a streaming service, or even a teacher), but they're actually scammers trying to steal your information. If something feels

off, it probably is—don't click or share until you're sure it's legit.

2. **Data breaches** are the online equivalent of someone breaking into your locker and rummaging through your stuff. Hackers target companies, steal sensitive info, and sell it to the highest bidder. Staying informed about these threats is crucial for dodging cyber bullets and keeping your information safe.

3. **Malware** includes planting viruses (nefarious computer software programs) onto your digital device (phone or computer).

4. **Social Engineering attacks** are when scammers try to trick you into giving up personal info—like passwords or credit card numbers—by pretending to be someone you trust. It could be through a fake text, email, phone call, or social media message. Instead of hacking your computer, they're "hacking" your brain by playing on emotions like fear, curiosity, or urgency to get you to click, share, or reveal something you shouldn't.

SIMPLE SECURITY PRACTICES TO PROTECT YOUR FINANCIAL DATA

So, how do you become a cybersecurity ninja?

- **Watch What You Click!** The best way to protect yourself from a malicious link is to make sure you don't click on any. Even if you feel confident the link in question is valid, the only way to be 100 percent sure you're safe is not to engage.
- **Use Strong Passwords!** Start with strong, unique passwords. And no, "password123" won't cut it. Get creative! Mix letters, numbers, and symbols like you're making a secret code only you know. Use a password vault app such as RoboForm, 1Password, or LastPass.
- Regularly **update software** and apps because outdated tech is like leaving your front door wide open for cyber crooks.

Software updates usually include fixes to close security holes within these systems.

- It's also wise to **keep an eye on account activity**. Spot anything fishy? Report it immediately—it's like calling security on a shoplifter before they make off with the goods.
- **Browse Carefully.** When accessing personal or financial information, ensure you are on a secure site (http**s**). The **s** after http tells you the site is secure.

LOCK IT DOWN: WHY MULTI-FACTOR AUTHENTICATION MATTERS

What is MFA?

Multi-factor authentication adds an extra step to logging in. It's not just your **password** anymore—it's something *more*. Usually, it combines **two or more of the following**:

- **Something you know** (like a password or PIN)
- **Something you have** (like a phone or a security code sent via text/app)
- **Something you are** (like a fingerprint or face scan)

Even if someone steals your password, they still can't get in without that second (or third!) factor.

Why It's a Game-Changer for Your Finances

Your money and identity are valuable. Hackers love to target bank accounts, Venmo, PayPal, and even shopping apps where your card is saved. They can drain your money, make fake purchases, or even steal your identity if they get in.

But with MFA turned on, even if they *guess or steal* your password, they hit a wall. No backup code? No entry.

Simple Ways to Turn on MFA

1. Go to your account's **security settings**
2. Look for **"Two-Factor" or "Multi-Factor Authentication"**
3. Choose how you want to verify—text, app (like Google Authenticator), or biometric (face/fingerprint)
4. Set it up and test it!

It's quick. It's free. And it can save you from a financial nightmare.

Hackers and scammers are out there daily, trying to trick people into giving up personal info, passwords, or bank details. But now you know better. You're building a digital shield around your finances by using strong passwords, turning on two-factor authentication, avoiding sketchy links, and staying alert to scams. You've got the knowledge—now it's time to use it. Stay sharp, stay safe, and take control of your digital world. Your future self (and your wallet) will thank you.

In this ever-evolving digital landscape, staying one step ahead of cybercriminals is key. Just as you'd double-check that you've got your keys before leaving home, ensure your online practices are airtight. Remember, you're not alone in this fight. A whole community of cybersecurity enthusiasts is eager to share knowledge and strategies. Forums and online groups offer support and advice, making it easier than ever to fortify your digital defenses. Engage with them, ask questions, and learn from others' experiences. The more you know, the better you'll be equipped to protect yourself digitally.

Reference Cybersecurity resources at reputable companies or government agencies, such as FINRA.org or America's Cyber Defense Agency (CISA), for tips on how to best protect yourself. Educating yourself is your secret weapon in the cybersecurity battle. Following updates from cybersecurity experts helps you stay informed so you can, too, sharing tips and tricks to keep your data locked up tight.

Pro Tip: When checking out resources to dig deeper, know that any website ending in .org means this is a not-for-profit agency. And .gov means this is a government agency.

So, whether you're gaming online or shopping for the latest sneakers, cybersecurity is vital. Your digital life deserves the same level of protection you give your offline life—maybe even more! So stay alert, stay informed, and most importantly, stay safe in the vast expanse of cyberspace.

Now that you've learned how to budget smart, save with purpose, invest wisely, and keep your financial info safe, you're not just managing money—you're building a solid foundation. But there's more to the story. It's time to take everything you've learned and start aiming higher. Up next, we'll dive into what it means to achieve **financial freedom**—where your money works for *you*, not vice versa. Let's go!

$$ LEVEL UP MONEY MOVES $$

1. ☐ Security Measures Checklist

- **Ensure applications implement data encryption:** Encryption is a secure vault for protecting sensitive and personal information.
- **Regularly update passwords:** Change them frequently and use two-factor authentication to bolster security measures.
- **Diligently monitor application permissions and privacy settings:** Stay vigilant and regularly review settings to safeguard your data effectively.
- **Check your Multi-Factor Authentication** settings for your financial apps

11

ACHIEVING FINANCIAL INDEPENDENCE

SETTING YOURSELF UP FOR SUCCESS: FINANCIAL PLANNING FOR TEENS

Setting financial goals is kind of like planning out your future on purpose. Like you'd make a playlist that sets the mood for a long drive, your financial goals help guide where you're headed. Each goal—whether it's saving for a car, college, or a side hustle—is a step toward building the life you want. Financial planning gives you a clear path forward, helping you use your money in ways that matter to you. It's about getting intentional, staying focused, and making wise choices that turn your dreams into real possibilities.

Whether your goal is accumulating funds for your first car or charting a course for a transformative gap year adventure, this plan acts as your compass. It diligently keeps you from wandering aimlessly into the unpredictable wilderness of hasty, ill-conceived financial decisions. So, what are the steps to build this nearly magical map? Start by envisioning and setting realistic, achievable goals. These might range from saving for an upcoming concert to investing in a top-notch laptop. By articulating these goals in writing, you create a tangible picture of what you wish to achieve.

Next, scrutinize your current financial standing. Do you have a windfall from a recent birthday tucked away? Excellent! Perhaps you've secured a part-time job and are earning a regular income? Even better. Recognizing what's in your virtual piggy bank provides clarity on how you can progress toward your goals. From there, you can draft a comprehensive financial plan, akin to sketching a treasure map where "X" marks the financial destination. As you make your way through life, this blueprint will adapt and evolve with changes in your circumstances and aspirations.

A thorough financial plan encompasses several critical moving parts. Let's initially delve into budgeting and strategic saving techniques. Your budget operates similarly to a dietary regimen, but with your wallet as the primary focus. By meticulously tracking your income and expenditures, you gain invaluable insights. Set aside a portion of your earnings, steadfastly earmarked for saving, because life's unexpected moments, such as urgent expenses, have an uncanny way of catching you unprepared. Then there's the consideration of investment planning and asset allocation. However, this might initially sound like something tailored for the financially initiated; picture it as sowing seeds today to savor the fruits in the future. By diversifying your investments, you manage risks effectively and amplify opportunities for future growth.

The allure of financial planning lies in its pivotal role in fostering long-term success. A carefully structured plan can propel you toward financial security and independence, equipping you with the freedom to make decisive choices, unburdened by the specter of financial constraints. When life throws a myriad of curveballs your way—such as unexpected expenditures or unforeseen shifts in income—your plan should possess the flexibility to adapt. Continually monitoring your progression is crucial, akin to regularly consulting your GPS to ensure you're on the right journey, making prudent adjustments whenever necessary.

THE IMPORTANCE OF FINANCIAL RESILIENCE: BOUNCING BACK FROM SETBACKS

Imagine yourself stepping into the shoes of a superhero, not donning a flowing cape, but enveloped in the powerful aura of resilience. This isn't your stereotypical superhero ability, yet it is undeniably critical in the grand tapestry of navigating life's unpredictable adventures, particularly regarding finances. Financial resilience acts as your metaphorical shield, an unwavering capacity to rebound when life decides to pitch curveballs in your direction. It is the stabilizing force in your financial world, standing firm even amidst an economy grappling with its tempestuous tempers. It's about your inherent ability to recuperate from the hiccups along your financial journey, maintaining equanimity even when confronting tumultuous times. Setbacks are universal companions on this journey—unexpected expenses, unforeseen job losses, or market downturns. However, with resilience as your ally, these hurdles won't hold you back long. Instead, you'll rise, brush off the dust, and forge onward, poised and prepared to handle whatever challenges await.

Building financial resilience requires a proactive and preventive mindset, akin to a navigator charting a course through potentially stormy seas with foresight and vigilance. One key strategy in this endeavor involves diversifying your income streams—think of it as assembling a harmonious choir with multiple backup vocalists; if one falters, the overall melody still rings true. This could mean embarking on a side hustle, engaging in a part-time job, or even capitalizing on the nostalgia surrounding your treasured collection of vintage video games. Additionally, an indispensable tactic on this front is crafting an emergency fund, a financial reservoir that serves as a safeguard during turbulent times. Imagine it as having a sturdy umbrella at the ready during an unforeseen downpour; you might not depend on it daily, but its presence is indeed a saving grace as stormy clouds gather. By diligently setting aside a modest portion of your earnings, you can cultivate a robust safety net, cushioning the impact should life's unpredictabilities jolt you off balance.

Financial setbacks resemble unanticipated guests arriving at your festive soirée, demanding acknowledgment while audaciously tweaking the party playlist to their preference. Such challenges possess the potential to momentarily sidetrack your meticulously crafted financial goals, albeit they need not completely unhinge them. Responsiveness and adaptability are pivotal, perhaps requiring a recalibration of your savings plan or deferring a significant purchase to a more opportune time. Importantly, these experiences harbor invaluable lessons; every mistake unveils a hidden opportunity, giving you wisdom and equipping you for more astute financial decisions.

Amidst the turbulence, a positive mindset emerges as a concealed yet potent weapon in sustaining resilience. It's all too easy to succumb to discouragement when plans go awry, but maintaining focus on long-term aspirations ensures that your gaze remains steadfastly fixed on the ultimate prize. Picture it as journeying through an enveloping fog; the immediate path may be blurred, but the promise of sunshine lies ahead. In addition, the practice of gratitude and mindfulness wields significant transformative potential. Regularly remind yourself of your accomplishments thus far and the resources accessible to you. These moments of introspective reflection fuel your motivation, anchoring you in positivity and optimism even amid challenging times.

You've just picked up the most talked-about video game of the season. The excitement is real, but without a solid walkthrough, you keep running into dead ends, confused by tricky puzzles, and defeated by tough bosses. Now imagine having an expert gamer by your side, someone who's been through it all, offering tips and guidance to help you level up faster and smarter. That's what financial mentorship is like. It's having someone who's already navigated the ups and downs of money management and is ready to share their experience—what worked, what didn't, and how to avoid common mistakes—so you can move forward with clarity and confidence.

Intrigued by the idea of financial mentorship? You might now wonder — how do you locate a good financial mentor? Begin by exploring your immediate surroundings at school or within your community. Teachers, coaches, or even that cool uncle who's always animatedly discussing stocks and market trends amid family gatherings might just possess the insights you're earnestly seeking. When choosing a mentor, carefully select those individuals who not only have a profound understanding of their domain but can also relate to your current stage in life's ever-evolving journey. Don't shy away from posing questions or reaching out via a humble email or an earnest chat at a school event. Networking might come across as a buzzword from the world of big business, yet at its core, it's simply about establishing meaningful connections with people who can support your growth. Keep in mind, mentors are not just poised to lecture or indoctrinate; they're more like your personal financial cheerleaders, energetically rooting for your success and celebrating your milestones.

Possessing a financial mentor will surely set you up for future financial success. A good mentor can be invaluable. They extend insights gleaned from their real-world experiences, offering you the cheat codes necessary to evade common pitfalls and maximize opportunities deftly. With their guidance, you're granted access to resources and knowledge that might otherwise take years to unearth on your own journey. Additionally, they may introduce you to others in their network, thereby expanding your horizons and opportunities exponentially.

However, amidst this scenario, don't underestimate the power harbored within peer mentorship. Sometimes, your fellow teens navigating similar trenches can offer the freshest perspectives and cutting-edge tips. Creating study groups or financial clubs with friends can transform learning into a thrilling, shared adventure. Discussing experiences and strategies with peers cultivates a robust sense of camaraderie, while sharing tales of triumph and missteps can unveil unexpected insights. Everyone must learn how to manage money, so don't be shy about discussing financial concepts or asking others what they have learned. Those who've discovered the latest and most innovative ways to boost their financial literacy are often eager to share their knowledge with others.

CONTINUOUS LEARNING: KEEPING UP WITH FINANCIAL TRENDS

The financial world constantly evolves, presenting the newest ideas and tools. If you want to stay ahead, you have to stay informed. The world of money is continually changing, with the latest tools, apps, and ideas popping up all the time.

Staying informed about these trends isn't just for Wall Street wizards; it's crucial for anyone looking to make smart money moves. Adapting to shifting financial landscapes helps you make informed decisions, keeping your wallet ahead of the game. Whether discovering the latest investment opportunity or avoiding an outdated practice, **continuous learning** ensures you're not left behind in the financial dust.

Reliable financial education doesn't require a secret map or a code word. It's all about knowing where to look. The internet is brimming with resources, but you need to sift through them like a pro detective. Start with online courses, Podcasts, or webinars. Websites like **Coursera** or **Khan Academy** offer courses ranging from budgeting basics to advanced investing strategies. Podcasts are another treasure trove of knowledge—imagine listening to financial advice while jogging or commuting. **The MoneyWi$er** podcast is an outlet for teens to have their questions answered about money. Books on personal finance are also a great place to obtain insights from experts who've been through the trenches and have come out wiser.

Staying informed enhances your decision-making skills in ways you might not expect. New investment opportunities often arise from emerging trends, and being in the know means you can seize them before they become mainstream. Conversely, clinging to outdated practices is like insisting on using a flip phone in the age of smartphones—effective once, but now hilariously obsolete. Continuous learning allows you to spot these opportunities and avoid old habits that no longer serve you well.

Financial apps and platforms have become more than just tools for tracking expenses—they're also educational powerhouses. Apps like **Mint** or **Robinhood** offer educational content right at your fingertips, breaking down complex concepts into digestible bits. **Virtual workshops** and **seminars** connect you with experts worldwide, bringing insights straight to your screen without you having to leave the comfort of your couch.

Incorporating financial education into your routine can be as simple as scrolling through social media. Follow influencers and economic experts who share tips and trends regularly. Even a five-minute read can open up new perspectives or reinforce your understanding of core concepts. Think of it as adding new spices to your culinary repertoire—it enriches the flavor of your financial knowledge and keeps things fresh and exciting.

As you navigate through life's financial maze, remember that staying informed is your secret weapon. The more you learn, the more equipped you become to make informed choices that align with your aspirations and goals. It's about staying curious, asking questions, and embracing new information with open arms.

In the ever-evolving landscape of personal finance, resilience transcends mere survival; it heralds an untapped potential to thrive in the face of adversity. It is about fortifying yourself with the tenacity required to adeptly maneuver through life's financial rollercoasters, exuding confidence and clarity at every turn. By nurturing resilience, you are preparing not just for life's uncertainties but also empowering yourself to lead a life wherein financial challenges serve not as defining boundaries but as enhancing milestones, enriching your journey toward holistic prosperity.

In a world where change is constant, being proactive in your financial education ensures you're not merely reacting to shifts but anticipating them. Whether it's mastering new technology or understanding market dynamics, continuous learning keeps you agile and ready to tackle whatever comes your way. Embrace this journey of discovery as an ongoing adventure—a thrilling quest where each new insight is a clue leading you closer to financial mastery.

With every piece of knowledge you gather, you're building a fortress of financial wisdom. This isn't just about acquiring facts; it's about cultivating a mindset that embraces change and growth. It's about transforming challenges into opportunities and turning uncertainties into stepping stones toward financial empowerment.

So stay curious, stay hungry for knowledge, and keep exploring the vast landscape of financial trends. Your future self will thank you for it!

INSPIRING STORIES: TEENS WHO ACHIEVED FINANCIAL INDEPENDENCE

Meet Emma, a teen entrepreneur whose story sounds like it belongs in the latest blockbuster movie. At just 16, she launched a handmade jewelry business from her bedroom. With a little creativity and a lot of determination, she started selling her designs online. It wasn't long before her unique pieces caught the eye of influencers, leading to a surge in demand. By the time she graduated high school, Emma had saved enough to cover her college tuition—a feat that left her friends in awe and her parents beaming with pride. Then there's Jake, a teen investor who turned his love for technology into a thriving portfolio. Armed with research and a keen eye for trends, he invested in tech stocks that skyrocketed, allowing him to fund his own college education and even start a side hustle.

So, what do these success stories have in common? It's not just about having a brilliant idea or being in the right place at the right time. Successful teens like Emma and Jake exhibit **discipline** and **perseverance**, sticking to their goals even when the going gets tough. They also embrace innovation and creativity, finding new ways to navigate financial pursuits. Whether it's launching a business or investing wisely, these teens aren't afraid to think outside the box and take calculated risks. Their stories serve as a testament to what can be achieved through grit and ingenuity.

Dream It, Fund It: Your Financial Goals Start Here

In this unfolding journey toward financial independence, it's crucial to remember that having a plan isn't about imposing constraints on your freedom. Instead, it's about empowering yourself with a myriad of choices. It's about being proactive, not reactive, ensuring that money serves your interests rather than the alternative. By thoughtfully crafting a financial plan, you're laying the groundwork for a future where you possess the reins of your destiny, prepared to navigate through the complex tapestry of financial opportunities in a world that is yours for the taking.

But how can you apply these lessons to your own life?

- Start by setting ambitious yet achievable goals, like saving for a trip abroad or launching a small business.
- Break these goals into smaller, manageable steps to avoid feeling overwhelmed.
- Leverage available resources, such as online courses or local entrepreneurship programs, to gain knowledge and skills.

- And don't underestimate the power of networking; connecting with like-minded peers can open doors to opportunities you never knew existed.

Remember, success isn't just about reaching the finish line; it's about the journey and the growth you experience along the way.

So, as you embark on your own financial adventure, draw inspiration from those who've walked the path before you. Learn from their triumphs and setbacks, embracing their strategies while adding your unique flair. Who knows? One day, your story might be the one sparking inspiration in others, encouraging them to reach for their dreams and achieve financial independence.

To wrap up Chapter 11, we looked at how real-life examples can inspire you to take charge of your financial future. You learned why setting money goals matters and how staying curious and always learning gives you a major advantage. Discipline and creativity play a big role too—they help turn small steps into big wins. As you work toward financial independence, remember this: **your journey is just beginning, and you're the one writing the story!**

"If you want to be financially free, you need to become a different person than you are today and let go of whatever has held you back in the past."

— ROBERT KIYOSAKI

---

1. ☐ **Reflection Exercise:**

Reflect on what you have learned throughout the course of this book. Revisit a time when you encountered a financial setback.

---

a. *What **insights** did that experience impart?*

_____

_____

_____

b. *How did it inform and **reshape your approach** to managing your finances?*

_____

_____

_____

c. *Jot down **three actions** you **executed well.***

_____

_____

_____

d. *Jot down **three actions** you **would revise** should similar circumstances arise.*

_____

_____

_____

This reflective exercise metamorphoses past adversities into pearls of wisdom, paving the way for informed, strategic decisions in the future.

2. ☐ <u>Create your Financial Goals Roadmap.</u>

Grab a blank sheet of paper, your digital notes app, or a white-board. Compose a list containing three short-term financial goals you intend to achieve within a year.

SHORT-TERM GOALS (To be achieved within a year)

_____

_____

_____

LONG-TERM GOALS (Realization greater than a year)
Estimate the monetary requirements for each goal and deter-mine how long you will need to save up. Break this down further into monthly savings targets, creating manageable steps. Contemplate your existing financial habits and deliberate on potential changes you could implement to successfully hit these targets. This insightful exercise will allow you to chart your course toward financial independence visually.

LONG-TERM GOALS	Cost	Action Steps Toward Goal
1.	$	1. 2. 3. 4. 5.
2.	$	1. 2. 3. 4. 5.
3.	$	1. 2. 3. 4. 5.

3. ☐ __Find a mentor using a Visual Mentor Map__

Get creative and construct your personalized "Mentor Map." Illustrate a prominent circle in the center designated as "Me." Surround it with various potential mentors—teachers, family members, friends—each housed in their own distinctive bubble. Use connecting lines to vividly demonstrate how each individual might assist you in reaching different financial goals. Consider annotating with notes on what each person might offer in terms of valuable experience or specialized knowledge. This engaging exercise will help you visualize your network and pinpoint who might be your optimal guides along the unique path to financial independence.

In life's unpredictable game, having mentors is akin to employing well-proven cheat codes for success. Whether they're seasoned pros who've navigated these waters before or fellow novices like yourself, mentors lift the burden of navigating finances alone. They're the guiding stars that shed light upon shortcuts and detours, ensuring that your journey is not only enlightening but genuinely enjoyable, filled with opportunities for growth and personal achievement.

4. ☐ __Research and subscribe to__ Financial Literacy newsletters, Audiobooks, or Podcasts for continuous learning

CONCLUSION

You've made it to the end—and that's no small thing. Throughout this book, you've built a foundation many adults wish they had. Understanding how money works gives you a major edge in life. It's not just about dollars and cents—it's about choices, freedom, and control over your future.

We've covered everything from budgeting and saving to investing, credit, debt, taxes, and insurance. You now know how to build smart money habits, avoid common pitfalls, and use financial tools to your advantage. These aren't just skills—they're life changers.

Here are the key takeaways:

- Create a budget and start tracking your money
- Start saving and investing early.
- Make a plan and stick to it—even when it's hard.
- Use digital tools to track and manage your money.
- Make smart decisions, not just for now, but for your future.
- Stay informed, stay flexible, and keep learning.

Technology is constantly re-shaping how we handle money, and you're in the perfect position to grow with it. The tools are right at your fingertips, from budgeting apps to investment platforms. Use them wisely.

But financial literacy isn't a one-time lesson—it's a lifelong mindset. Keep asking questions. Keep seeking out reliable information. Whether it's through articles, videos, podcasts, or mentors, never stop learning.

Now it's your turn to act. Set real financial goals—big or small. Start now, whether it's saving for something important, building an emergency fund, or exploring how to invest. The earlier you begin, the more options you'll have.

And don't go it alone. Share your knowledge with friends, join school clubs or community groups, and build a support network. The more you engage, the stronger your financial confidence will grow.

Thank you for committing to this journey. Your effort to understand money and take control of your financial future is powerful. You have what it takes to be independent, informed, and financially successful.

You're not just prepared—you're ready. You've Got This! Keep making smart choices, stay curious, and keep **leveling up — one $$ money move $$ at a time**.

REFERENCES

- *Financial Literacy: What It Is, and Why It Is So Important To ...* https://www.investopedia.com/terms/f/financial-literacy.asp
- *Money-Saving Apps for Teens: Budgeting, Tracking, and ...* https://www.azcentralcu.org/blog/money-saving-apps-for-teens/
- *Teaching Kids About the Magic of Compound Interest* https://www.moneygeek.com/financial-planning/compound-interest-for-kids/
- *Checking vs. Savings Accounts: The Difference* https://www.nerdwallet.com/article/banking/checking-vs-savings
- If Following a Budget Is Hard, Do This Instead – Wise Ol' Crow. https://wiseolcrow.com/if-following-a-budget-is-hard-do-this-instead/
- *4 Best Budgeting Apps for Teens in 2025 - WalletHub* https://wallethub.com/answers/b/budgeting-apps-for-teens-2140878684/#:~:text=The%20best%20budgeting%20apps%20for%20teens%20are%20Acorns%20Early%2C%20BusyKids,set%20allowance%20and%20spending%20limits
- *Budgeting Tips for Teens in 6 Easy Steps - Better Money Habits* https://bettermoneyhabits.bankofamerica.com/en/personal-banking/teaching-children-how-to-budget
- *Digital Budgeting for Teens: Guide to Managing Money* https://news.shib.io/2025/04/01/digital-budgeting-for-teens-intro-to-managing-money/
- *How to Budget by Cash Stuffing Envelopes* https://www.ramseysolutions.com/budgeting/envelope-system-explained?srsltid=AfmBOooxmiLcbx6gEfIRoU8Q2-8ie6TIkVp8RM6IqZFOB6bCAG2jDXAS
- *Money Math for Teens: The Emergency Fund - Finra Foundation* https://www.finrafoundation.org/sites/finrafoundation/files/2024-10/the-emergency-fund_0.pdf
- *What Are The Best Tools For Tracking Financial Goals?* https://www.bccu.org/blog/what-are-the-best-tools-for-tracking-financial-goals
- *The Power of Compound Interest: Calculations and ...* https://www.investopedia.com/terms/c/compoundinterest.asp
- *Fun and Unique Savings Challenges for Teens* https://www.chevronfcu.org/articles/post/chevron-blog-posts/2024/08/22/fun-and-unique-savings-challenges-for-teens
- *5 Apps To Help Teens Start Investing* https://www.forbes.com/sites/robertberger/2022/05/08/5-apps-to-help-teens-start-investing/
- *Benefits of Compound Growth - Schwab MoneyWise* https://www.schwabmoneywise.com/essentials/benefits-of-compound-growth#:~:text=Compound%20interest%20makes%20your%20money,from%20those%20investments%20grow%20together.

- *How to Invest in Stocks: 2025 Beginner's Guide* https://www.nerdwallet.com/article/investing/how-to-invest-in-stocks
- *The Importance of Diversification* https://www.investopedia.com/investing/importance-diversification/
- *8 Ways to Help Your Teen Build Good Credit Now* https://www.experian.com/blogs/ask-experian/how-to-help-your-teen-build-credit/
- *Best Student Credit Cards Of 2025*
- https://www.forbes.com/advisor/credit-cards/best/student/
- *Debt Management Strategies | Office of Student Loans ...* https://personalfinance.duke.edu/student-loans-101/debt-management-strategies/
- *11 Credit Myths Debunked - Experian* https://www.experian.com/blogs/ask-experian/credit-myths-vs-facts/
- *Tax Basics for Teens: Filing Your First Tax Return*
- https://blog.taxact.com/taxes-for-teens-filing-your-first-tax-return/
- *Understanding Auto Insurance for Teenagers* https://www.kitchellaw.com/blog/auto-insurance-for-teenagers.cfm
- *IRS Free File: Do your taxes for free*
- https://www.irs.gov/filing/irs-free-file-do-your-taxes-for-free
- *Health Insurance Basics (for Teens) | Nemours KidsHealth* https://kidshealth.org/en/teens/insurance.html
- *Why Millennials, Gen Z Are Likely to Use Mobile Banking ...* https://www.cnbc.com/select/why-millennials-gen-z-use-mobile-banking-apps/
- *The Gig Economy: Opportunities and Challenges for Teens* https://www.flytotheworld.org/blog/jgrtjb3lksj6ybr577rn4ntjwks22d
- *9 Best Banking Apps and Debit Cards for Kids and Teens* https://www.nerdwallet.com/article/banking/buzzy-banking-apps-for-kids-and-teens
- *Cybersecurity Best Practices*
- https://www.cisa.gov/topics/cybersecurity-best-practices
- *Money Smart for Young People*
- https://www.fdic.gov/consumer-resource-center/money-smart-young-people
- *14 Teen Entrepreneurs and How They Succeeded*
- https://www.oxford-royale.com/articles/14-teen-entrepreneurs
- *Four (4) Tips for Building Financial Resilience in Young People* - https://www.creditsmart.co.za/four-4-tips-for-building-financial-resilience-in-young-people/
- *Mentoring Youth About Finance: Empowering the Next ...* https://bbbsli.org/financial-literacy-mentorship-for-youth/
- *Ramsey Solutions' "Budgeting Apps Comparison 2025,*
- https://www.ramseysolutions.com/budgeting/budgeting-apps-comparison?srsltid=AfmBOopAsyk3nB2twX84DfLp1x60v8IpzKPq5m9_FkIt EH5iAHbkriCD
- *How to Choose Health Insurance: Your Step-by-Step Guide*
- https://www.nerdwallet.com/article/health/choose-health-insurance?msockid=14fa12cb0e7360002974002d0f746198

- *Take Care of Your Loved Ones With Health Insurance*
- Get Health Insurance Quotes From RamseyTrusted Experts - Ramsey
- Debt Payoff Calculator - Stress Proof Your Money. https://stressproofyourmoney.com/tag/debt-payoff-calculator